ADVANCE

KOSSOYE: A VILLAGE LIFE IN ETHIOPIA

"A remarkably comprehensive, concrete and, especially, empathic study. Strongly recommended reading for those interested in Ethiopia, as well as for those interested in the present and further expected problems in the development of rural areas of the so-called third world countries. The impact of the currently dominant type of globalization, mainly economic and capitalistic, is clearly presented and discussed by the authors."

> — Louis Molineaux, author (with G. Gramiccia) of *The Garki project* (World Health Organization, 1980)

"Through recounting their lifetime attachments to Ethiopia, Andrew and Dennis Carlson outline the evolution of modern health care in Ethiopia. For those of us trying to be students of as well as active participants in the Ethiopian health system, the accounts in the book approximate an extended form of our professional biography. What intrigues me is that population remains a critical issue in the country's socio-economic development today as it was identified by Dennis in the 1960s, in addition to the ironical fact that we still do not have proper interventions in place."

> — Damen Haile Mariam, M.D., Ph.D., Addis Ababa University

Kossoye

THE NORTH GONDAR REGION

KOSSOYE

A VILLAGE LIFE IN ETHIOPIA

Andrew J. Carlson
and Dennis G. Carlson

The Red Sea Press, Inc.
Publishers & Distributors of Third World Books

P. O. Box 1892   **RSP**   P. O. Box 48
Trenton, NJ 08607   Asmara, ERITREA

The Red Sea Press, Inc.
Publishers & Distributors of Third World Books

| P. O. Box 1892 | **RSP** | P. O. Box 48 |
| Trenton, NJ 08607 | | Asmara, ERITREA |

Copyright © 2010 Andrew J. Carlson and Dennis G. Carlson
Second Printing 2010

Book and cover design: Saverance Publishing Services

First Published by Addis Ababa University Press, 2008.
ISBN 978-99944-52-12-5

Library of Congress Cataloging-in-Publication Data

Carlson, Andrew J.
 Kossoye : a village life in Ethiopia / Andrew J. Carlson and Dennis G. Carlson.
  p. cm.
 Includes bibliographical references and index.
 ISBN 1-56902-323-9 (cloth) -- ISBN 1-56902-324-7 (pbk.)
 1. Ethnology--Ethiopia--Kossoye. 2. Rural development--Ethiopia--Kossoye. 3. Economic development--Ethiopia--Kossoye. 4. Kossoye (Ethiopia)--History. 5. Kossoye (Ethiopia)--Economic conditions. 6. Kossoye (Ethiopia)--Social life and customs. I. Carlson, Dennis G. II. Title.
 GN650.5.E8C37 2010
 305.863--dc22

                           2009045166

For

Krista

and

Beulah

TABLE OF CONTENTS

❖ ❖ ❖

TABLES AND MAPS

❖ ❖ ❖

Tables

Maps

PREFACE

❖ ❖ ❖

On a Friday morning in October 1963, students and teachers from the Haile Sellassie I Public Health College and Training Centre were dropped by the side of the road, about twenty-eight kilometers north of the historic city of Gondar in northwest Ethiopia. They were greeted by men, women, and children who lived in several hamlets, perched at the edge of the Amhara plateau, at an altitude of 2,900 meters. After brief introductions, students asked residents about their health problems. They mentioned frequent respiratory infections, intermittent diarrhea, and skin rashes, but the most important problem was dirty water. The hamlet of Zinjero Wuha, ("baboon water" in Amharic, the national language), contained the one spring that was the main water source for the larger parish community known as Kossoye. But the spring was shared with livestock and the wild animals living along the edge of the escarpment. When asked why they needed clean water, one of the farmers responded: "To make better *tella* [a local beer] for Sunday morning parish meetings."

As they rode back to the College that afternoon, students and teachers engaged in a heated discussion about whether it was essential to first teach the local people that the germs causing diarrhea were in the water. Dennis Carlson, the new co-director of the College, suggested that the most important fact was that the community wanted a protected water source. "Why" did not really matter at this point so much as that the community saw the desirability of clean water and a relationship with the College.

So began this globalization drama in rural Ethiopia. The Kossoyans offered local perspectives and problems. The students and staff from the Haile Sellassie I Public Health College and Training Centre, members of a growing middle class, brought a national viewpoint and their modern expertise. The expatriate professionals, on the scene as a result of government-to-government and non-governmental programs in North America and Western Europe, offered another set of theoretical and international perspectives.

This book, based upon research conducted over a period of 44 years, brings together the work of the authors (father and son) and many students, staff, and faculty members from the University of Gondar. Dennis Carlson went to Ethiopia first in 1958 and has worked in the country as a physician, administrator, and professor. From 1963 until 1967 he made weekly visits to Kossoye, with students from the College and often with young Andrew in tow. In 1974 he returned for a brief visit, as the country was entering a period of revolutionary change. After 17 years in the United States, in 1986 Carlson returned to work in Ethiopia, but although he traveled to Gondar many times, it was not until 1993 that he was able to visit Kossoye, as it was off-limits to international travelers. In 1994 Andrew proposed to Dennis that they write a history of Kossoye. Over the past fifteen years the authors (usually alone but sometimes together and with family and colleagues) have made regular visits to Kossoye, for research and various development/service projects. In eight chapters (summarized below) the authors narrate and analyze forty-four years of local-national-international interaction and cooperation.

Chapter one begins in the years after the Second World War, when under United States influence Emperor Haile Sellassie advocated a Western development agenda that focused on building an educated middle class for employment in a modern state administration. In the 1960s the urban, middle class grew dramatically, as did the expatriate population of teachers and other professionals. An unanticipated result was that the new modern Ethiopians became serious critics of the Emperor and his conservative feudal society.

Chapter two returns to the globalization drama, as students and faculty of the Haile Sellassie I Public Health College and Training Centre interact with and learn about the Kossoyans. The Kossoyan ancestors, among the original Agew inhabitants of Northern Ethiopia, had lived in the area for generations before the 17th century when the city of Gondar was built as the national capital. In the 1960s, even as peasants within a feudal society, Kossoyans enjoyed substantial local control and autonomy. Household heads lived with their children and other family members in small, thatched, waddle and daub homes. They distinguished between the poor and rich. Most household leaders (men and women) were interested in improving their lives but not in taking risks with their land or animals. Most families had 10 or 12 children and thought of their progeny as a source of pride and security.

Chapter three is about leadership in Ethiopian society and more locally in Gondar and Kossoye. One of the major dramas in Kossoye was the emergence of Taye Wubineh as an innovator. During a period of twelve months in 1965 and 1966 he built a rectangular house with a metal roof, started the first public school, and planted eucalyptus trees as a cash crop. Remarkably these developments happened within months of a visit to Kossoye from Haile Sellassie and Queen Elizabeth II. Why did these local events follow the Imperial visits so closely? Did the inspiration for innovation come from local, national, or international actors? These were the questions in the 1960s.

Chapter four examines the health transition (declining infant mortality and population increase) that spread over the world in the twentieth century. Most scholars locate the beginning of the health transition in Ethiopia in the 1930s, well before the Haile Sellassie I Public Health College began its extension services in Kossoye. But the College contributed to the health transition in Kossoye and many other rural communities by providing basic public health and medical services. In 1967 the College responded to requests from local women for family planning assistance (and five individuals were fitted with intra-uterine contraceptive devices).

Chapter five tells the story of the Revolution of 1974-1991, which ended the Solomonic monarchy and feudalism. Kossoyans had their land nationalized, fundamentally altering notions of wealth and family connection. The relationship between the College and the community was disrupted by revolution and war. The local people experienced wrenching social engineering, especially in the villagization campaign of 1987 which brought new families to the area and solidified the Cherema and Zinjero Wuha hamlets' position as a government center for the larger parish community. Kossoyans also lost dozens of sons and husbands to the war with Eritrea.

Chapter six is about the ethnic dilemma Kossoyans faced in 1991. Since at least the 17th century, when Gondar became the national capital, the Orthodox Christian Church and the Amhara ethnic group had been assimilating the traditional Agew peoples, including the Kossoyans' ancestors, who were primarily from the Kemant ethnic group. After the fall of the Derg and the beginning of the new EPRDF led government, however, Ethiopia was reconstituted as an ethnic federation, opening a dialogue on the possibility of a Kemant restoration. Failed efforts at political mobilization convinced most Kossoyans who were ethnic Kemant that their grandparents' language and culture were beyond recovery.

Chapter seven is about the population crisis in Kossoye and Ethiopia, from the perspective of Kossoye's agricultural families. Since 1963 population in Cherema and Zinjero Wuha has increased from 125 people to more than 1300. As a result family cultures built around agriculture and land inheritance have been dramatically changed. While one or two sons are often designated to farm and take care of the parents, parents now send some of their sons and most of their daughters to school because they cannot give them land to farm. Land shortage is related to demonstrable increases in rates of malnutrition since the 1960s.

Chapter eight looks at the recent conflict between the traditional and modern Kossoyans as they contemplate their futures. The first six families who settled in the area in 1945 came from Sisomedir, only a kilometer away, because they wanted to be on the new Gondar road, built in 1937 during the brief Italian occupation. Sixty-three years later, Kossoye is a multi-ethnic urban center serving highland and lowland rural populations. It has electricity, television, radio, and cell phones. It boasts one of the best schools in the district, a health post, five wells, administrative buildings, a police station, and storage facilities. There is talk that a Kossoyan who made his fortune working in China will soon build a hotel, at the edge of the escarpment, on the exact spot where Haile Sellassie entertained Queen Elizabeth II in 1965. The chapter concludes with an assessment of how the past forty-four years of local-national-international interaction have affected the Kossoyans and a suggestion of possible remedies.

We believe this local, longitudinal study illuminates challenges faced by millions of the rural poor around the world. The global health transition that reached Ethiopia in the 1930s established the necessary conditions for the population to grow from less than 10 million to more than 80 million by 2007. We hope the Kossoye story will help answer questions about how rural communities around the world can improve the quality of their lives while meeting the challenges of high population density and land shortage.

The historical sources used in this study are the result of reflective practice and reporting by many people over a period of 44 years. Three generations of environmental health students, beginning in 1963 and continuing to the present, have drawn maps and compiled demographic censuses. Over the years several generations of students and faculty from the College have conducted interviews and written reports. The early work of Alemayehu Abraha, Mulugeta Mengistu, and Tadelle Mengesha has been especially helpful in writing the early chapters of this book. Hundreds of photographs (only a fraction included here) provide a visual record of changes in Kossoye. Data on school enrollments beginning in 1965 demonstrate changing patterns of gender relations, as well as the increasing popularity of education. Health and nutrition reports and analyses, including student papers presented at local conferences, inform the longitudinal analysis of local health conditions.

None of these sources would have been available without the cooperation of the people in the Kossoye parish community who welcomed us into their homes and consented to endless questions on often personal topics. We are especially grateful to Taye Wubineh, his son, Kes Sisay Taye, and his grandchildren for their generosity and support over the past 44 years. Faculty and students from the Haile Sellassie I Public Health College and the Department of Community Health, now part of the University of Gondar, have been active participants in much of the research. We could not have completed this work without the help and friendships of Ato Amsalu Feleke, Ato Tibebu Kassa, Ato Melkie Endris, Ato Molla Tafete, Ato Abdul Kader, Professor Yigzaw Kebede, Professor Yared Wondim-kun, Ato Gizatchew Ashagre, Dr. Mansur Osman, Ato Getu Degu Alena, Dr. Mogus Tiruneh, Dr. Mengesha Admassu, Dr. Getnet Mitike, Dr. Mesresha Abuhaye, Dr. Mesfin Addisie, Dr. Mesganaw Fantahun, Dr. Melake Berhan Dagnew, and Sister Asefash Gebru. Other friends who have helped us in Gondar are Ato Telele Desta, Ato Temesgin Sereke-Birhan, Ato Makonen Sereke Birhan, Ato Tegegne Abdul, Ato Binyam Eyob, and Ato Seifu Wolde Abraham.

At The Red Sea Press, Kassahun Checole and Angela Ajayi have been a pleasure to work with. We owe special thanks for very helpful comments from two anonymous readers and the Director of the Addis Ababa University Press, Professor Mesresha Fetene. We also thank Louis Molineaux and James L.A. Webb, Jr. for careful readings and helpful suggestions. In addition, Dr. Asfaw Desta, Dr. Ayele Meshesha, Dr. Frank Doden, and Louise F. Carlson read drafts and saved us from many errors of style and substance. Dennis Carlson owes a debt of gratitude to Karl-Eric Knutsson, Sven Rubenson, George M. Foster, Frederick C. Gamst, and Carl E. Taylor. Saba W. Masho has given invaluable assistance in statistical analyses. David and Joyce Veterane provided financial assistance for completion of a health and nutrition survey. Andrew Carlson acknowledges two grants from Capital University which helped fund research and travel in Ethiopia. He is grateful for the encouragement of colleagues and students at Capital University, especially Richard Ashbrook, Denvy Bowman, Elizabeth Cook, Jody Fournier, Robin Johnson, Basil Kardaras, Andrea Karkowski, Tonda Lazofson, William Lorson, Suzanne Marilley, Thomas Maroukis, Emily Morris, Sharron Ogutu, Tanya Poteet, Heather Pritchard, Brian Wallace, and Michael Yosha. He has also benefited from association with students and faculty in the International Studies Program at the Ohio State University, particularly Anthony Mughan.

Our families have allowed us to spend many months away from home. We thank Beulah Downing, Krista Magaw, Anna Magaw Carlson, Jim and Bonnie Magaw, Louise F. Carlson, Rebecca Carlson, Marilou Carlson, and Steven G. Carlson for their love and continuous encouragement. While our goal has been to provide as accurate a history as possible, we alone are responsible for errors of fact and judgment.

Andrew J. Carlson, Yellow Springs, Ohio
Dennis G. Carlson, Bainbridge Island, Washington
September 2009

CHAPTER ONE

THE DEVELOPMENT AGENDA

❖ ❖ ❖

Following the Second World War Ethiopia was at a critical juncture in its history. While poor in comparison to countries in Western Europe and North America, it seemed to have good prospects for modernization. The country had a Great Tradition with historic connections to classical Greece and ancient Persia, a core cultural myth about King Solomon and the Queen of Sheba, a church-state history beginning in 330 C.E, and a history of writing and ox-plow agriculture extending more than 2500 years. In the 1960s Ethiopia had a highly regarded monarch who not only had been in power since before 1930, but who was part of the Solomonic dynasty. The population of about 15 million in 1950 was modest but sufficient for economic development. The land was presumed to have the potential to make Ethiopia the "Breadbasket of Africa." By reunion with Eritrea, colonized by Italy in the 1880s, Ethiopia also regained its base on the Red Sea coast, which, when combined with its railroad route from Addis Ababa to the then French colony of Djibouti, provided full access to international markets.[1]

Ethiopia had an advantageous historical and international position. During medieval and renaissance periods in Europe, kings and military leaders planning crusades to "liberate" Jerusalem from Islam hoped to make an alliance with "Prester John," the mysterious Ethiopian Emperor of the Orient who was Christian.[2] For centuries, Ethiopia was considered "off limits" to Europeans trying to establish African colonies because of this Christian tradition. The Italians, who came late in the 19th century to the "Scramble for Africa," disregarded these precedents. In 1896, under the leadership of Emperor Menelik II, Ethiopian armies repelled the Italian colonial army, making Ethiopia the only African state to avoid colonization and causing Italy to become the "laughingstock" of Europe. Consequently, Ethiopia had the opportunity to negotiate on nearly equal terms with European colonial powers in the establishment of modern era state boundaries, which extended the country's territory southwards and westwards far beyond the historical origins of classical Abyssinia.

In 1936, after the Italians again invaded, Emperor Haile Sellassie made his famous speech to the League of Nations in Geneva, pleading for help in defense of his country's sovereignty. At the time neither the British nor the Americans appreciated the threat from aggressive governments in Germany, Italy, and Japan, and so they did not lend Ethiopia any assistance. But when Italian fascists under Mussolini joined the Axis Alliance in 1941, the British helped the Ethiopians expel the Italians as part of their larger wartime strategy in Africa. When the Japanese attacked Pearl Harbor later that same year, the United States became fully committed to the Allied war effort.

The Second World War reorganized alliances in virtually every region of the globe. Most African states would achieve independence from European powers in the 1960s, but Ethiopia's historic independence and participation in the war put it in an advantageous bargaining position, especially compared to other African states. Haile Sellassie negotiated a reunion with the former Italian colony of Eritrea, which had been an integral part of classical Abyssinia. In 1963 he also became the first president of the Organization of African

Unity, and Addis Ababa, the home of new OAU headquarters, functionally became the capital of Africa. Thus Ethiopia became a strategically important test case in the Cold War debate over paths to modernization and development.

After the Second World War the prospects for Ethiopian modernization were better, perhaps, than they had ever been. Haile Sellassie had international support that would provide an array of resources. He had leverage with wealthy allies. He had the Cold War ideological contest between communists and capitalists that made Ethiopia, for the West, a test case to prove the superiority of their approach to modernization and development.

A Feudal Society

The questions were whether and how modernization and development could proceed in a traditional feudal society. In *Wax and Gold: Tradition and Innovation in Ethiopian Culture* (1965), Donald N. Levine provided a sociological analysis of Ethiopia in the late 1950s and early 1960s. He described Ethiopia as "a gate through time to a state of being that is richly medieval."[3]

In the Amhara Orthodox Christian culture of central and northern Ethiopia, power, land, and status were distributed unevenly to five distinct classes. At the very top was the Emperor, an "elite of One." Theoretically "He" (and the Higher Power) owned all the land in the country.[4] He enjoyed the imprimatur of the Solomonic dynasty, providing the Biblical authority of a lineage that extended from King Solomon and the Queen of Sheba. From this came the Emperor's full title, "Lion of Judah, Elect of God, King of Kings." He was an absolute ruler with vast powers, theoretically.

Below the Emperor was the nobility (*makuannent*). Although they did not inherit titles, which were all conferred by the Emperor, they did inherit land, the most important

3

asset in a feudal agricultural society. Land was the *sine qua non* for power and status. When the center did not hold (that is, when the empire dissolved into separate kingdoms) nobles often asserted authority in their regional domains. Indeed, becoming Emperor of Ethiopia usually involved asserting the power of the empire through the subjugation of competing aristocrats and kings.

For most of Ethiopian history, imperial power originated in the northern and central Ethiopian provinces of Tigray, Gondar, Welo, and (since the 19th century) Shewa. Most nobles from these areas lived in local or regional camps, managing their lands, collecting taxes from peasants, and, from time to time, providing military or other services to the Emperor and other allies. A small group operated nearer to the Emperor, connected through patronage and, sometimes, marriage to the royal family. This was a feudal society prone to fragmentation and shifts in boundaries, depending on alliances between local and regional aristocrats whose primary identities tended to be as warriors.[5] In the European colonial era, between 1880 and 1910, state boundaries became more formalized. Thus the persistent argument over the past 50 years about the "nationality question": is Ethiopia an empire created by colonialism or is it a unified whole, an evolving multicultural society?[6]

In the modern era of Ethiopian history, beginning in 1855, the emperors were more successful in limiting the nobility's powers. One of Haile Sellassie's strategies, developed in the 1930s and reinforced in the 1955 Constitution, was to order peasants to pay land taxes directly to his Ministry of Finance rather than to the local lords. This had the effect of diminishing the nobility's access to revenue, reducing its power over the peasantry, and strengthening the center.[7]

The second most privileged class was the clergy (*kahenat*). The clergy's authority rested principally in the church, which maintained the legitimating mythologies for the Ethiopian state, and in church lands, estimated to cover at least 15 percent of the country's arable land.[8] As with the nobility, clerical spheres were both local and national. For centuries the archbishop (*abuna*) was appointed from the Alexandrian Patriarchate in Egypt. Hence the highest ranking person in the Ethiopian Orthodox Church was almost always an Egyptian with little knowledge of the national language or culture. In 1958 Haile Sellassie was successful in winning the church's independence from Alexandria, removing this affront to Ethiopian sovereignty. Henceforth the fifteen archbishops of the Ethiopian Orthodox Church, located in the 14 regions and in Jerusalem, were "subject to the approval of the Emperor...."[9] As the first leader of the state and first leader of the Ethiopian Orthodox Church, Haile Sellassie achieved an unprecedented level of unity in state-church authority and an added title: "Defender of the Faith."[10]

The vast majority of clerics had local roots, as they were drawn from the ranks of the nobility and the landed peasantry. The primary socializing institutions were the Ethiopian Orthodox church schools, where tens of thousands of young males studied reading, scriptures, and church literature. This education prepared them for minor roles as deacons and priests. Most priests also farmed family lands. Church office brought additional prestige and freedom from taxes. The priests at the top of the local church hierarchies enjoyed extra income from ritual functions as well as the use of church land and labor. Some clergy had power and privileges similar to those of the nobility.[11]

The Emperor was sensitive to competition from the Ethiopian Orthodox Church, since the church had exerted serious constraints on monarchical authority many times in the past. The 1955 Constitution proscribed clergy from offering judicial remedies for temporal offenses. Churches were denied the right to corvée labor on church lands, which often went to support the clergy.[12] Of course the imperial government did not have the means to enforce these laws, so implementation was sporadic.

The peasant class was numerically the largest group in Ethiopian society. In 1960 there were approximately 19 million peasants, more than 90 percent of the total population. These were Ethiopia's producers, who raised or made most of the goods that supported the leisure classes (nobles and clergy). Peasants with the highest status owned land and sometimes held governmental positions which "merged imperceptibly into the lower stratum of the nobility." Peasants who did not own land worked as laborers or servants, a status below landowners. At the bottom of the peasant group were the "weavers, minstrels, common soldiers, and beggars."[13]

Traders made up the fourth class of Ethiopian society. Importers with shops held a higher status than peddlers who went from door to door, market to market. Wealthier Christian Amhara and Tigrayan merchants also had higher status than Arabs, Armenians, and Muslim Ethiopians. As with the wealthiest peasants, the status of wealthy Amhara and Tigrayan merchants approached that of the nobility.

Below the merchants, in a caste-like status, were artisans (potters, tanners, metal smiths). These individuals often came from minority ethnic groups such as the Gurage and the Bete Israel (also known, pejoratively, as Falasha). At the bottom of the social order were the slaves or descendants of slaves, usually from the western and southern borderlands. They often worked as house servants or laborers.

There were ethnic and regional dimensions to this social order. In northern and central Ethiopia, the Orthodox Church was the predominant religious institution. In the south and east, Islam was the major religion, and languages were more diverse. Southern and Western Ethiopians, notably the Oromo, the single largest ethnic group in the south-central part of the country, were more distant from the Amhara culture and less well represented among clergy, nobility, or peasantry (although quite strong in the military). Thousands of Oromo were victims of slave-raiding parties.

Tens of thousands had land confiscated by Amhara nobles who received grants from Emperor Menelik II as a reward for military service. In the southeast, the Somali residents of the Ogaden were uncommitted to Ethiopian national identity. In the northeast, Eritreans were divided on Ethiopian national identity. On the western border in Gambela and Gamo Gofa, ethnic groups were probably unaware of whether they were Ethiopian, Sudanese or Kenyan.[14]

In short, the feudal society still present in the 1960s reflected an Amhara and Tigrayan culture which had been ascendant since early medieval times. These two culture groups made up about a third of the whole population of modern Ethiopia defined by boundaries that Menelik II negotiated with European colonial powers. Some of the eighty-odd ethnic groups (such as the Oromo, Kemant, Bete Israel, and Gurage) found places in the Amhara social order or were assimilated into the dominant culture.[15]

Educating a Middle Class

One obstacle to a modernization premised on national unification was that some groups did not feel that they were Ethiopians. Another obstacle was that Ethiopia had virtually no middle class of educated professionals who could serve as administrators, teachers, physicians, engineers, lawyers, salesman, and military officers.

The first government school in Ethiopia was established in 1908 in Addis Ababa by Emperor Menelik II. Levine estimates that "some six to seven hundred boys and girls received the beginnings of a modern education in the government schools of Addis Ababa by 1935." Other children were educated in provincial and foreign mission schools. Forward momentum was lost during the five years of Italian occupation, when many educated Ethiopians were executed. But after Liberation, enrollments in government schools increased steadily: to 25,000 by 1944; 60,000 by 1950; and 243,000 by 1963. A small fraction of all children in government schools (a total of 7,250 in 1958-59) were at the secondary level.[16]

The first colleges and technical schools opened after the Second World War. The first was a Red Cross Nursing School in Addis Ababa which accepted its first students in 1949. In the 1950s the government sponsored six colleges devoted to arts and sciences, agriculture, engineering, public health, building, and national defense. The first class at University College in Addis Ababa, taught by Jesuit faculty members from France and Canada, was graduated in 1954. In 1958-59 the total national enrollment in post-secondary education was 760 students, a small fraction of the college-age men and women in the country.

The Public Health College and Training Centre in Gondar began classes in October 1954. The College's major support came from the Ministry of Public Health, the World Health Organization, UNICEF, and the United States bilateral assistance agency, then called "Point Four," now known as USAID. The staff members working in the World Health Organization and UNICEF wanted to help usher in a new age for health in developing countries. UNICEF was able to provide financial support for bold initiatives that would promote health for children. The United States government was committed to international development programs and was highly supportive of WHO and UNICEF. Together they promoted ideas, strategies, and technologies considered most effective in rural peasant communities.

The World Health Organization was established in 1948 on the premise that good health cannot be achieved merely by treatment of illnesses, but also requires prevention of disease and active promotion of health. The founders believed that health status is fundamentally shaped by social, political, economic, and cultural dynamics, not only biological or other physical causes. Thus to control and eradicate root causes of illness, it was held to be essential that several types of health personnel work together in collaboration with community members. At the mid-point of the twentieth century, Ethiopia provided an excellent opportunity to train health personnel for complementary roles in service teams.

The Haile Sellassie I Public Health College and Training Center in Gondar took an approach to education based on what was then state-of-the-art public health policy and practice. A key strategy, developed specifically within the Ethiopian context, was training interdependent teams of health professionals to provide curative care and extend preventive and promotional services in communities. Health center team members made regular visits to schools, markets, prisons, and households; conducted health education activities; provided immunizations; and made sure their environmental health measures were carried out. Mapping and census-taking were essential prerequisites in facilitating outreach programs. Protection of water supplies and disposal of waste materials around homes and villages were critical to prevent water and food-borne diseases. Improved housing, particularly the control of smoke from interior cooking fires, was necessary to reduce respiratory conditions. Special emphasis was placed on improving mother and child care at home. Community nurses also were available for deliveries at home under the supervision of trained midwives.

Until the early 1960s the Emperor took a personal approach to students, providing free room and board at secondary schools and colleges, thus ensuring that students understood their dependence on him. Many students retained a profound sense of gratitude to the Emperor. Yet students had conflicting loyalties, especially as they were socialized into professions that emphasized expertise and merit. Moreover, those who traveled abroad to North America and Europe for higher education became aware of Ethiopia's relative poverty and backwardness.

In December 1960 impatience with the pace of the Emperor's modernization plans resulted in an attempted coup. While Haile Sellassie was in Brazil on a state visit, a small group of educated officers led by the Neway brothers initiated a change in government, naming the Crown Prince, Asfa Wossen, as the new monarch. Germame Neway received BA and MA degrees in the United States from the University of Wisconsin and Columbia. His brother Mengistu was educated in the military and was a member of the Black Lion organization, formed during the resistance to Italian occupation. While in the 1950s the Black Lions supported Haile Sellassie as well as an agenda of national political and economic reform, the Neway brothers were convinced that aristocratic corruption, which the Emperor tolerated, obstructed modernization. This sentiment was shared by residents in urban areas (high school and university students, teachers, government employees, taxi drivers, and merchants), some of whom participated in public demonstrations in support of the coup.

The Emperor cut short his state visit to Brazil and entered Addis Ababa as a superficial normalcy returned to the country. The Neway brothers were executed. Criticism of the Emperor was discouraged. Students who had participated in the demonstrations were required to write personal notes of apology. But the illusion of a personal connection between the Crown and the middle class faded as the Emperor became more distant and less paternalistic towards students. The sheer scope of the educational mission, involving thousands of expatriate teachers and tens of thousands of students, also contributed to the estrangement from the Emperor of the emerging middle class.

The formation of the United States Peace Corps in 1961, conceived as a strategy for improving American international relations and advancing the causes of democracy and capitalism, offered up a steady stream of young American volunteers.[17] Ethiopia received the largest of any of the national Peace Corps contingents, indicating the country's favored status and the fact that it was considered a relatively secure place.[18] Other countries from the "West," including Israel, Japan, and Taiwan, also created volunteer organizations on the U.S. Peace Corps model. These organizations were conceived as a massive public relations campaign to woo Third World nations toward the "West" rather than the "East." Young volunteers, helping in the fields of education and development, were the soft side of the Cold War. Many U.S. Peace Corps volunteers taught in Gondar in the high school and the Public Health College.[19]

Inevitably, unintended consequences resulted from the association of young American teachers with young Ethiopian students. These teachers, even if they admired the Emperor, encouraged their students to see modernization (especially the American version) as a desirable goal. The historian Elizabeth Cobbs Hoffman argues that the mission of western volunteer organizations was to "spread the message of economic development and international 'good will.'"[20] Of course, as Ethiopian students learned about social and natural sciences, they developed comparative perspectives on their own country that were not always favorable.

Thus the peril of Haile Sellassie's focus on building a new middle class: students were being educated to want a changed society. The country's major constituent groups (the peasants, clergy, and nobility) were often resistant to change. Educated young people wanted change to come quickly, in their lifetimes. Conflicts large and small were the result.

Development work in rural Ethiopia did not promise the sort of life to which students aspired. Most came from traditional peasant communities. They wanted to help rural people. But they also expected to live in more modern, urban sectors of Ethiopia—in Addis Ababa or, possibly, in a regional urban center. A problem for the faculty members would become how to spark commitment to improving the quality of peasant life, especially when this required significant personal sacrifice.

The Expatriate Professionals

While some social scientists studying Ethiopian development appreciated these tensions, most of the expatriate professionals coming to Ethiopia in the 1950s and 1960s were focused on narrow objectives: delivering health services, teaching secondary school and college students, and building institutions.[21] Dennis Carlson's journey was not much different from those of other expatriates, except that as a result of his family history in impoverished rural Sweden he sympathized with Ethiopian peasants. His own father worked as an indentured servant in peat bogs in Sweden, until at the age of 18 in 1913, when he migrated to the United States.

For most of his first five years in Ethiopia, from 1958 to 1962, Carlson was the only physician at the Swedish-American Baptist hospital in Ambo, in west-central Ethiopia. The experience of trying to provide health care for a population of a half million people in the catchment area surrounding the hospital led to some insights into the needs for Ethiopian human resource development. Reading Benjamin Paul's *Health, Culture and Community* (1955) provided new insights about health care delivery, especially how social science concepts and theories can serve as tools for understanding and implementing effective health programs.[22] Since it did not seem practical to train a cohort of physicians with western-style medical education, given the constraints of resources and the immediate needs, Carlson turned to the fields of community and public health. In Ambo, very soon after his arrival, he began training dressers and other hospital personnel to practice disease prevention and promotion of health as well as curative care.[23]

In 1962, after completing a five-year term as a medical missionary, Carlson left Ethiopia for study at the School of Public Health at the University of California in Berkeley, then beginning a new Behavioral Sciences Division. He was

one of the first two graduate students under the mentorship
of Andie L. Knutson, a leading social psychologist,[24] and
also had the opportunity to study with George M. Foster,
a pioneer in medical anthropology. Foster emphasized the
importance of understanding the historical roots of health
cultures and the necessity of a multifaceted approach to community development. His research with Mexican peasants
provided a model of longitudinal research among traditional
rural people.[25] This approach became Carlson's inspiration
for the early work in Kossoye in the 1960s.[26]

In California Carlson was exposed to a set of theories,
concerns, and questions about improving health care in
traditional societies. George M. Foster's paper, "What is a
Peasant?," was in a reader on peasant society that included
many leading anthropologists of the mid-twentieth century
including Robert Redfield, Clifford Geertz, Oscar Lewis,
Eric Wolf, and Sidney Mintz.[27] His longitudinal research,
Tzintzuntzan: Mexican Peasants in a Changing World (1967),
examined the social structures, religions, relationships, economics, demographic changes, and histories of this rural
population. He described a culture where the peasant world
view was characterized by notions of "limited good": that
one person's advantage comes at another's disadvantage.[28]
In a labor-intensive and cash-poor community, Foster
concluded, individuals tried to maintain economic equality
through various ritual and social obligations, which tended
to discourage innovation and individual achievement.

These works provided a framework for thinking about
rural culture in Ethiopia. Most of the social scientists writing
in the field emphasized the conservative nature of "peasant
societies." Whether in Southern Italy, Mexico, or Ethiopia,
rural peoples lived on the fringes of the industrialized world,
supporting themselves through agriculture and daily labor,
much as their ancestors had done. Their utter dependence on
weather and the soil focused their attention on the natural
world and created a sense of fatalism about the vicissitudes

of life. Death, illness, injury, or a poor harvest could devastate a family and leave children destitute. This fundamental insecurity and marginality made rural farmers conservative. They did not feel that their precarious position allowed any risk-taking behavior that modernizers might propose.

These scholarly debates on rural society extended to reflection on development and modernization. Strategies included improving access to education and communication, encouraging local institutions, facilitating out-migration, enhancing state support in times of family crisis, and using exemplars of modernity such as middle class outsiders living in a traditional village for several years.[29] Most of these scholars presumed that integration into a modern global economy provided the surest path to improvement, defined in terms of Western criteria.

While there were those who were not optimistic about the prospects for change in these traditional rural communities, particularly in the context of cultural resistance to modernization,[30] the work of David C. McClelland provided ideas on how to encourage innovation. In *The Achieving Society* (1961), McClelland explored the dynamics of motivation and leadership, suggesting that a key to encouraging change was identifying the local leaders most likely to be innovators.[31] The publication in 1965 of Donald Levine's *Wax and Gold: Tradition and Innovation in Ethiopian Culture* lent credibility to the focus on innovation and stirred considerable interest and controversy in Ethiopia, especially since it focused on high school and university students as possible vanguards of modernization.

One of Carlson's challenges was that he worked with two constituencies: middle-class professionals, whom he was responsible for educating, and rural farmers, who were in desperate need of public health services. As a non-Ethiopian health professional, he did not engage in the Ethiopian political debates of the day. He also did not foresee the serious chasms between the feudal regime and the new middle class.

His focus was on creating institutions that would deliver improved health services to rural Ethiopians.

Yet Carlson and other expatriates were aware of development politics. In 1964 the U.S. Ambassador to Ethiopia, Edward M. Korry, visited the Public Health College. Carlson recalled: "after we had our refreshments the Ambassador told me he would like to say a few words to the teaching staff. I don't remember all he said, but I clearly recollect his final thoughts. Korry said something to this effect: 'As you know, the United States government gives major financial and technical support to the Public Health College and the Agriculture University in Alemaya. We appreciate what you are doing, but you should know that our financial support is really only paying rent for use of Kagnew Station in Eritrea, where the U.S. has a telecommunications center for surveillance of the Middle East.'" Carlson went on to recall the dismay of Ethiopian and American faculty members, because "we had been operating under the assumption that the U.S. was sincerely interested and concerned for the well-being of the Ethiopian people." The result was that "any trust the faculty had in American collaboration and support was deeply shaken."[32]

Korry's pragmatic approach to development work reflected the realist politics of the day. In the context of the Cold War, Moscow, Beijing, Addis Ababa, Stockholm, and Washington, D.C. were all concerned with how to bring the traditional rural peoples (third- and fourth-world countries) into the industrial world (first or second).[33] This Cold War ideological divide reflected differences in social theory at mid-century. In the United States, the work of the German sociologist Max Weber informed a fundamentally cultural interpretation of modernization that emphasized the importance of religion and rationality in shaping economic behavior and capitalist institutions. This theory fit well with the then-popular theory of American "exceptionalism"—the notion that the religious beliefs of the American people account for the strength of democratic institutions, and that religious belief provides a foundation for economic prosperity. In the Soviet Union and China, the works of Marx and Engels provided a materialist interpretation of development that focused on class antagonism and abstract historical forces. In the 1960s, Ethiopians and their expatriate western colleagues tended to favor capitalist and Weberian theories, even if there were contradictions and confusions in the actual development agenda, because of Ethiopia's international alliances and the national status quo. But they were also aware of the success of Soviet and Chinese modernization and development efforts using a very different theory.[34]

At the time the dominant U.S. perspective on development was articulated by W.W. Rostow, an economic historian who also served as President Lyndon Johnson's Secretary of the Treasury. In *Five Stages of Economic Growth: A Non-Communist Manifesto* (1960), Rostow suggested that modernization could be replicated in traditional societies, presumably like Ethiopia.[35] He also suggested that such development followed five stages through which a society could be transformed from a traditional subsistence economy into a mass consumption society. Widely read and discussed, this book provided a map for how traditional rural societies might modernize according to the western plan. The slim paperback volume traveled widely, including to Gondar and the Haile Sellassie I Public Health College. While it is not clear that it made its way onto any of the faculty members' syllabi or reading lists, it can be said that Rostow's confidence about a program for capitalist development (and the ultimate goal of a mass consumption society) had much in common with the world view of American and Western European faculty members in Gondar.

The historian Harold Marcus argues that the Emperor's development plan made sense: focus on the creation of a middle class, expand commercial agriculture, strengthen government institutions and the constitution, and finally, increase industrialization.[36] Taken over time, these processes would produce surplus income that would allow new investments in urban businesses and industries. The fact that the Emperor assumed that Ethiopia was uniquely well suited to development through commercial agriculture was grounded in the then widely held belief that his country had the potential to be the "Breadbasket of Africa." The political dimensions of Ethiopian development were similarly assumed to follow what had become recognized as a classic Western pattern, with the monarchy eventually giving way to democracy. While the Emperor did increase the power of the central government, and therefore the power of the monarchy, the fact that he also engineered two new Ethiopian constitutions in 1930 and 1955 provided some progressive credentials. Indeed, much of the middle class dissatisfaction with the Emperor was not with the expansion of his powers or the monarchy, but rather with the continued strength of the nobility. For much of the 1960s, the Emperor was seen as a reliable custodian of Ethiopia's political development.

The work of the Swedish economist Gunnar Myrdal provided some contrast to the dominant Western views on development, because it offered a comparative perspective that emphasized differences in geography, politics, and history. Two works published in the 1950s were notable: *Economic Theory and Under-developed Regions* (1957) and *The Political Element in the Development of Economic Theory* (1953). These were followed by Myrdal's three-volume study of economic development, *Asian Drama*, published in 1968. One of the most important of Myrdal's observations concerned the impact that modern public health would have on population growth, and the unintended consequences this would then have for development efforts. As a result of contact with Myrdal's ideas, in 1963 and 1964 Carlson raised the issue about Ethiopia's high rate of population growth with other faculty members and students.

In retrospect, it is clear that there were many problems with the development agenda of the 1960s. It did not account for the long-term negative effects that the introduction of some development measures (public health, modern medicine) would have on population growth. It did not envision an agricultural future for peoples in rural areas. It did not predict the impact of political instability, both internationally and nationally, on the development agenda and its implementation.

Notes

1. This national history reflects careful reading of Paul B. Henze, *Layers of Time: A History of Ethiopia* (London, Hurst and Company, 2000); Harold G. Marcus, *A History of Ethiopia* (Berkeley: University of California Press, 1994); and Bahru Zewde, *A History of Modern Ethiopia, 1855-1991,* Second Edition (Addis Ababa: Addis Ababa University Press, 2002). The terms modernization and development are used in the intellectual and political context of the Cold War to denote the transition of agricultural and feudal societies (mostly in the so-called Third World) into industrial and democratic societies. These terms are ideologically charged, especially in the context described in this chapter, where so-called First World Western industrial democracies offered one vision of modernization and development while the Second World states offered another vision.

2. Francisco Alvares, *The Prester John of the Indies: A True Relation of the Lands of the Prester John: Being the Narrative of the Portuguese Embassy to Ethiopia in 1520,* trans. C.F. Beckingham and G.W.B Huntingford (Cambridge University Press, 1961): 4, 5, 34.

3. Donald N. Levine, *Wax and Gold: Tradition and Innovation in Ethiopian Culture* (Chicago: University of Chicago, 1965), ix-x.

4. The Emperor seemed sincere in his belief that he had been anointed by God to lead Ethiopia and had valid "divine rights." He led a devout Orthodox Christian life and acted as if God would protect and lead him. For example when he returned from Brazil in 1960

after an attempted coup he toured Addis Ababa in an open convertible seeming to have no fear that anyone would harm him.

5. Sven Rubenson, *The Survival of Ethiopian Independence* (London: Heinemann, 1976); Mordechai Abir, *Ethiopia, The Era of the Princes: The Challenge of Islam and the Reunification of the Christian Empire 1769-1855* (New York: Praeger, 1968), 31.

6. Examples are the opposing arguments in Donald N. Levine, *Greater Ethiopia: The Evolution of a Multiethnic Society*, 2nd ed. (Chicago: University of Chicago Press, 1974, 2000); and Bonnie K. Holcomb and Sisai Ibssa, The *Invention of Ethiopia: The Making of a Dependent Colonial State in Northeast Africa* (Trenton, NJ: The Red Sea Press, 1990).

7. Levine, *Wax and Gold*, 155-167.

8. Levine, *Wax and Gold*, 183.

9. Levine, *Wax and Gold*, 182.

10. "Defender of the Faith" was not the only title which connected him to the Judeo-Christian tradition. Rubenson traced the history of the phrase "The Lion of the Tribe of Judah" back to its original use in describing the Ethiopian emperor in the 16th century by the Portuguese. That its origin begins in the New Testament Book of Revelations, chapter 5, is not widely recognized. "The Lion of the Tribe of Judah, Christian Symbol and/or Imperial Title," *Journal of Ethiopian Studies*, vol. III, no. 2 (July 1965): 75-85.

11. Levine, *Wax and Gold*, 155-177.

12. Levine, *Wax and Gold*, 182.

13. Levine, *Wax and Gold*, 149.

14. Wendy James, "No Place to Hide: Flag-waving on the Western Frontier," in *Remapping Ethiopia: Socialism & After*, ed. Wendy James et. al. (Oxford: James Currey, 2002), 259-275.

15. In *Greater Ethiopia*, Levine identifies nine categories of ethnic groups: North Eritrean, Agew, Amhara-Tigrean, Core Islamic, Oromo, Lacustrine, Omotic, Sudanic, and caste groups. Each category contains many ethnic groups.

16. Levine, *Wax and Gold*, 108, 111.

17. Elizabeth Cobbs Hoffman, *All You Need Is Love: The Peace Corps and the Spirit of the 1960s* (Cambridge: Harvard University Press, 1998). See also, by the same author, "Decolonization, the Cold War, and the Foreign Policy of the Peace Crops," in *Empire and Revolution: The United States and the Third World since 1945,* ed. by Peter L. Hahn and Mary Ann Heiss, (Columbus: Ohio State University Press, 2001), 123-153.

18. Henze, *Layers of Time*, 257.

19. During the mid 1960s the Public Health College usually had four to six U.S. Peace Corps volunteers on the teaching staff.

20. Hoffman, "Decolonization, the Cold War, and the Foreign Policy of the Peace Corps," 125.

21. Donald N. Levine's *Wax and Gold* is an apt illustration, and it did get him in trouble with the Emperor, who went so far as to deny him an entry visa to the country. David C. Korten was on the faculty at the Haile Sellassie I University in the mid 1960s and later published *Planned Change in a Traditional Society: Psychological Problems of Modernization in Ethiopia* (New York: Praeger Publishers, 1972). Another American social scientist who researched the challenges of modernization was Frederick C. Gamst. See for example his works *The Qemant: A Pagan-Hebraic Peasantry of Ethiopia* (New York: Holt, Rinehart, Winston, 1969); and *Peasants in a Complex Society* (New York: Holt, Rinehart and Winston, Inc., 1974).

22. Benjamin D. Paul, ed., *Health, Culture and Community: Case Studies of Public Reactions to Health Programs* (New York: Russell Sage Foundation, 1955).

23. The Ministry of Health sponsored one and two year training programs for workers in hospitals and clinics. Though several nursing programs were established as well, the majority of health personnel were trained at a lower educational level as "dressers," mostly in hospitals staffed by missionaries.

24. Andie L. Knutson, *The Individual, Society, and Health Behavior* (New York: Russell Sage Foundation, 1965).

25. George M. Foster, "Fieldwork in Tzintzuntzan: The First Thirty Years," in *Long-term Field Research in Social Anthropology*, ed. by George M. Foster et. al. (New York: Academic Press, 1979), 165-184.

26. The longitudinal analysis took on more meaning in the 1990s when Dennis Carlson returned with his son, Andrew, a historian, to study how Kossoye had changed since the 1960s.

27. See Jack M. Potter, May N. Diaz, and George M. Foster, editors, *Peasant Society: A Reader* (Boston: Little, Brown and Company, 1967).

28. George M. Foster, *Tzintzuntzan: Mexican Peasants in a Changing World* (Prospect Heights, Illinois: Waveland Press, 1988).

29. George M. Foster, *Tzintzuntzan: Mexican Peasants in a Changing World*, 348 fn.

30. Banfield, *The Moral Basis of a Backward Society* (New York: The Free Press, 1958), 165-166.

31. David C. McClelland, *The Achieving Society* (New York: Irvington Publishers, Inc., 1976, 1961).

32. Email communication from Dennis G. Carlson to Andrew J. Carlson, July 24, 2006.

33. See for example Robert J. McMahon, "Introduction: The Challenge of the Third World," in *Empire and Revolution: The United States and the Third World Since 1945,* ed. Peter L. Hahn and Mary Ann Heiss (Columbus: Ohio State University Press, 2001), 1-14.

34. Bahru Zewde, *Pioneers of Change in Ethiopia: The Reformist Intellectuals of the Early Twentieth Century* (Addis Ababa: Addis Ababa University Press, 2002), 211.

35. W.W.Rostow, *The Stages of Economic Growth: A Non-Communist Manifesto* (Cambridge: Cambridge University Press, 1960).

36. Marcus, *A History of Ethiopia*, 164.

CHAPTER TWO

A RURAL COMMUNITY

✤ ✤ ✤

For the first six Friday visits to Kossoye in October and November 1963, students from the college worked with the local residents to protect the spring at Zinjero Wuha. The plan was simple. Locate the eye of the spring. Dig out the area. Build a protective steel-reinforced concrete box with a metal pipe through which water flowed by gravity into an area where household containers could be filled. There was no spigot, so run-off would proceed into a small stream bed over the edge of the escarpment.

On the day that a steady, clear stream of water began flowing through the metal pipe, a spontaneous celebration erupted. Men, women, and children from the nearby hamlets came to see the spring. Virtually all families benefited from the project. Now they had the essential ingredient for better beer (*tella*): clean, fresh water. As a result, *senbete,* the meeting after church on Sunday where people socialized and discussed community affairs, would be more enjoyable.

The improvement of the water source created a positive foundation for gaining the Kossoyans' trust. This was not an easy proposition, because despite the appearance that this was an entirely Orthodox Christian and Amhara community, the villagers in Cherema and Zinjero Wuha were in fact people of Kemant ethnicity, who had a fear of ridicule and exploitation after centuries of coexistence with the Amhara.

Villagers also worried that personal information would be given to the government and result in extra taxation.

The protected spring, however, provided evidence that a relationship with the college could be beneficial. Over time Kossoyans took students and faculty into their confidence and agreed to collaborate in a variety of projects including a census, mapping, a health survey, hyena control, and latrine construction. They also invited faculty members and students to the *senbete* meetings, a sign of acceptance into community life.

All of these projects were designed with several specific goals in mind. First, the Kossoyans' lives must be improved in practical ways that could also be replicated in other traditional rural communities. Second, students must have hands-on opportunities to learn about rural health delivery strategies and practices. Third, the local people themselves must be encouraged to engage in dialogue and actions to improve their lives. A guiding principle was that the Kossoyans control the agenda.

Within a year of work in Kossoye, students had made major headway in understanding the historical and cultural context of rural community life. Information came from many sources, and students often discussed their findings during the drives up to the village and back to the college.

The Ethiopian Orthodox Church

One early conclusion that would have been true of most rural communities in northern Ethiopia was that the major local institutional presence was the Ethiopian Orthodox Church. The parish answered to the regional church administration headed by an archbishop who lived in Gondar, and to the national church headquartered in Addis Ababa. It was one of thousands of rural Ethiopian Orthodox parishes in Ethiopia.

A map drawn by students in 1966 depicted "the Kossoye Parish Community" (*debir*). (See Map 1.) The focal points

Map 1. The Kossoye Parish Communities (1966)

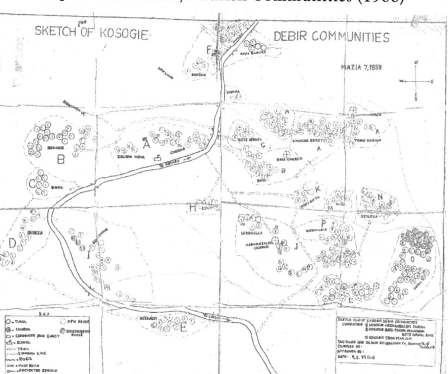

Source: This map of three parish communities was drawn in 1966 by
students from the Haile Sellassie I Public Health College and
Training Center.

were three churches surrounded by twenty-five hamlets,
thirty minutes to two hours from the road by foot. A fourth
church in Ambaras named Saint Michael was also officially
part of the parish but oriented itself towards Ambaghiorgis, the district market town and government center. A
fifth church down the escarpment was omitted, as were the
lowland hamlets. If one assumes an average of five residents
per household of the 368 houses drawn on the 1966 map
(Map 1), the total population of the parish was about 1,840.
If one also assumes that the fourth and fifth churches had

the same number of members as the others, the total estimated parish population would be close to 3,000 persons. The vast majority of these were farmers and their families. There probably were about 50 priests, deacons, and nuns in the parish, mostly members of local farming families.

The parish was also part of a network of local and regional governing institutions ultimately reporting to the Emperor. In 1963 the parish did not have any government units, unlike Ambaghiorgis, the district center eight kilometers north on the road. But it did have representatives such as the *atbia dagna* and *chika shum*. The *woreda* was part of a regional district or province, then called Begemder and Simen, headquartered in Gondar. The province and the *woreda* had representatives in parliament in Addis Ababa and in the Emperor's administration.

Table 2.1: The Parish Community in 1966

Hamlet	Households	Estimated Population
Keskazit	11	55
Bebeza	14	70
Digina	7	35
Sisomedir	26	130
Cherema/ Zinjero Wuha	25	125
Shebin/Koso Badima/Kiflay	25	125
Mesal	16	80
Gomenge	27	135
Kena	5	25
Bete Israel	6	30
Bata	15	75
Chincha Beret	26	130
Tsion Mariam	9	45
Serdegella	18	90
Awragy Sifta	5	25
Duriye	6	30
Workmidir	35	175
Serleha	20	100
Gura	46	230
1 unidentified hamlet	26	130
Total	368	1840

Kemant Culture

The fact that the primary political identity of the Kossoye hamlets was as a parish community indicates the close connection between church and state. But other historic identities remained, below the surface. Kossoye and the entire Gondar area lies within the historically Agew region of Ethiopia, extending from Lasta in the east to Lake Tana in the west, and to the Sudan border in the northwest.

The Agew languages are classified as Cushitic rather than Semitic (as are Amharic, Gurage, Geez, and Tigrigna). In his anthropological investigation, *The Qemant: A Pagan Hebraic Peasantry of Ethiopia* (1969), Frederick C. Gamst identified eight subgroups of the Agew: Kemant, Awiya, Kumfal, Hamir, Bilan, Damot, Hamta, and Falasha.[1] The Kemant zone, from Chilga to Kerker, covered an area of several hundred square kilometers. Kossoye is at the northeastern edge of the Kerker area. (See Map 2.) The Kemant zone also included Ethiopia's largest concentration of Falasha.

The Agew people's claim to land in Northern Ethiopia precedes the history of written language in the Horn of Africa. Anthropologists and historians consider the Agew the oldest culture in northern Ethiopia. According to Gamst, Bushmanoid and Caucasoid hunters and gatherers who occupied the Ethiopian plateau before 7000 BP [Before Present] "undoubtedly were the ancestors of the Cushitic-speaking peoples of present-day Ethiopia, including the Kemant."[2]

While evidence is conjectural, the Agew are associated with the beginning of agricultural society in the Horn of Africa, dating perhaps to 5000 BP or earlier. Over time, use of ox-plow technology resulted in greater food production, which then allowed population growth. By 3000 BP the Agew dominated Ethiopia and began expanding southward. As a result they became, in Taddesse Tamrat's words, "the

Map 2. The Kemant of Ethiopia

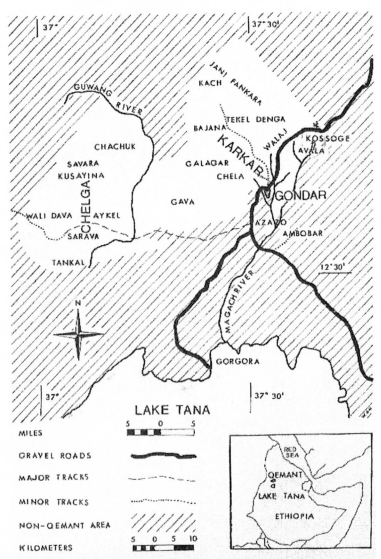

Source: From *Gamst. The Qemant, ie.* 1969 Wadsworth, a part of Cengage Learning Inc. Reproduced by permission.

very basis on which the whole edifice of Aksumite civiliza-
tion was constructed."[3] One of the distinguishing character-
istics of Agew culture, ox-plow farming, remains standard
practice in Kossoye and the surrounding highlands.

A remaining mystery about the Agew groups, notably
the Bete Israel and the Kemant, is the origin of their Hebraic
culture. One explanation suggested by Kemant and Bete
Israel oral traditions is that their ancestors came to Ethiopia from Egypt and Palestine. Taddesse recounts that this
narrative depicts the Agew as descendants of "Adil, son of
Yitrham and grandson of King David of Israel. He accompanied his cousin, Menelik I, on his way back from Jerusalem
and was assigned to settle in and rule over Lasta....It is from
here that all Agew dispersed in various directions."[4]

Another story of origins with less historical scope says
that the Agew groups are descendants of the seven sons of
Aydarki and Anzakona. Three went to Lasta, two to Gojjam,
and two to Kerker. Among the Kemant there is a story that
Aydarki had two additional wives, Semendara, the mother
of the Agew of Simen, and Feinabahura, the mother of the
Falasha. Of the original seven sons, Kadasti and Keberwa
moved to Kerker. Keberwa had nine sons, two of whom,
Gadhu and Bathu, "acquired the Kemant lands from a king
of the Falasha Agew who gave them as much land as they
could ride across on horseback before sunset. Gadhu stopped
the sun for three days to increase the amount of land that
could be acquired in this way."[5]

Gamst identified an oral tradition extending fourteen
generations to the Kerker *wambar* (a priest king) and seventeen generations to the Chilga *wambar*. Calculating twenty
years per generation, this would place the beginning of the
genealogical history of the Kemant in the early to mid 17th
century, the beginning of the Gondarine dynasties. This, of
course, leaves considerable historical time between what was
remembered of the genealogical tradition and the oral tradition claiming descent from Canaan, Ham, and Noah.

While historians have debated the value of these narratives, the paucity of evidence has left room for several sketchy hypotheses. One thesis is that Agew peoples adopted elements of Hebraic religion through contact with immigrants, perhaps from Yemen, between 2500 and 1000 BP. Immigration from Saudi Arabia may have brought more sophisticated agricultural technology as well as written language and dry stone masonry. Over time, the interaction and intermarriage between Agew and South Arabian groups created what Gamst calls the "proto-Amhara or Ethiopic groups."[6]

Another thesis locates the origin of the Hebraic elements of Agew culture within the past one thousand years. In this argument the Agew peoples adopted alternative narratives of Hebraic origins in order to differentiate themselves from the growing influence of the Orthodox Christian, Tigre-Amhara culture.[7] The appeal of this thesis is that it fits better with the Kemant genealogical traditions noted above.

The Kemant claims to connection with Egypt presents a mystery. It is notable that the pre-Christian era word that Egyptians had for themselves was "KMT."[8] This contains all the consonants in the word Kemant, providing some possible evidence for the theory of early Egyptians migrating to Ethiopia. How else would the Kemant have known to call themselves Kemant, given their reliance on an oral tradition?

Gamst argues that until the twentieth century the Kemant maintained their culture more successfully than other Agew groups. One explanatory factor is that "religion helped the Kemant to survive as a distinct ethnic group despite centuries of acculturative pressure from the surrounding Amhara." In Gamst's view the strong Kemant boundaries were a result of the "largest pagan substratum" in the "northern and central parts of the Ethiopian high plateau."[9]

A second explanation, suggested by the linguistic scholar Zelealem Leyew, is the isolation of Kemant people, especially in the remote western valleys of Chilga.[10] The people of Kossoye, like other Kemant in the Kerker area (which includes the city of Gondar) were significantly less isolated than the Chilga peoples. By 1963, virtually all had given up their traditional language and religion for the Amhara language and Ethiopian Orthodox religion. They had become, with the creation of the modern Ethiopian state, "ethnic Kemant," aware that Haile Sellassie was their leader and that they were Ethiopians.

As early as 600 years ago in the Kossoye area, Amhara Christian society had been assimilating smaller nonliterate Agew peoples. The first Orthodox Church in the Kossoye parish, Tsion Mariam, was built in the 13th century during the reign of Atse Adiam Seged Iyasu. The second church, Bata Mariam, was built in the 17th century during the reign of Atse Tekle-Giorgis, soon after the establishment of Gondar as the national capital. Major trade routes from Ethiopia to Sudan passed through the Chilga-Kerker region. Especially during and after the building of Gondar in the 17th century, the Ethiopian crown relied on Kemant peoples for support as soldiers, bureaucrats, and palace help. In the late nineteenth century, Emperor Yohannes IV of Tigre instigated a major campaign to convert Muslims, Falashas, and Kemant to Ethiopian Orthodox Christianity. In the 1890s Menelik II allowed the Muslims and Falashas to return to their faiths, but the Kemant, who had no written tradition, were not included in the royal dispensation.

Even so, Kemant culture remained viable in the Kossoye and Kerker area until the middle of the twentieth century. The most dramatic turning point came in 1958/59, as a result of a visit that Haile Sellassie made to Gondar. Confronted with the fact that many of the Kemant followed a different religion, the Emperor encouraged Layke-Mariam Birru to undertake a mass conversion campaign among the Kemant people. Although it was Layke-Mariam's intention only to convert Kemant to Orthodox Christianity and not to damage their language, Zelealem Leyew reports that damage, in fact, occurred. Kemant people still understand their ethnicity to be defined both by religion and language. Use of Amharic as a primary language typically followed conversion to Christianity and Amhara self-identification.[11] In other words, becoming Christian was assumed to mean becoming Amhara, which necessarily meant speaking Amharic.

Kinship, Ethnicity, and Religion

The earliest census and mapping of Kossoye took place in 1964 (Map 3). This document shows that twenty-two families and 120 people lived in the Zinjero Wuha and Cherema hamlets. One elder, Guangul Zeleke, reported "that all the people...are interrelated either by marriage or by blood."[12] This kinship homogeneity was the rule in the hamlets, with the exception of two or three individuals brought into the group through marriage and/or slavery. Neighboring hamlets included Amhara Orthodox Christians and Bete Israel.

The original patriarch of the hamlet residents was Melke, who probably lived sometime in the early nineteenth century in the area of Ambaras, four kilometers north of Kossoye. (This is based on the calculation that a family tree extending seven generations would cover a period of about 140 years, or 20 years per generation.) The story told to both Alemayehu Abraha and Mulugeta Mengistu (with some variations, discussed below) is that Melke came from Gojjam.

Melke's first and head wife was known as Enqueye and came from the lowlands. He subsequently married Gonnad Dengule. She herself, or her family before her, had come into the area from Selawin Abbo in Lasta.[13] The story told to Mulugeta by another elder, Tagele Wubineh, is that all were descendants of Gonnad of Lasta, Melke's second or third wife. Tagele reported that all the majority group members in Cherema and Zingero Wuha were descendants of the Mebeshin group (presumably one of her children).[14]

Map 3. Cherema and Zinjero Wuha, 1964

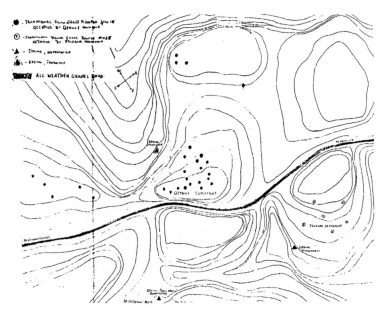

Source: Map drawn by students at Haille Selassie I Public Health College and Training Centre, 1964.

The genealogy presents several questions about the ethnic origins of Melke and Gonnad. Notably, Tagele recalled the mother, while Alemayehu's informant (probably Berihun Lemma) recalled the father, and that the mother, Gonnad, was a second or third wife and from Lasta. The evidence is incomplete but indicates a mixed marriage between an Amhara man and a Kemant woman. Lasta is certainly a location associated with the Agew, suggesting that Gonnad was Kemant. Melke served as the *chika shum*, the lowest level of government officialdom, evidence of assimilation into the Amhara Christian group, perhaps explaining how Melke's children acquired their extensive land rights and continued assimilation into the Amhara culture and the Ethiopian Orthodox Church. Some family members later held the title of *chika shum*, often awarded to wealthier peasants.

The connection to the lower rungs of the feudal aristocracy, which came from assimilation into the dominant Amhara group, provided at least a few family members social advantages. The *chicka shum* position combined elected and hereditary qualities. Typically the *chika shum* served terms of two years (although one served for 30 years) based on local approval. The privilege to occupy the position rested also on land holdings, explaining why it was possible for a *chika shum* to represent an area where he did not live.[15] Before the 20th century the *chika shum* also acted as a judge. Later this responsibility was delegated to a new position, that of the *atbia dagna*. Although low-ranking compared with regional or national elites, these local political roles afforded opportunities for the exercise of power and privilege.

The story of the arrival of Melke's progeny in the Kossoye area is confused, because people moved between inheritance property (*rist*) held in several locations. During the Italian occupation, 1936-41, Melke's descendants moved from the highland hamlet of Ambaras, four kilometers north of Kossoye, down into a lowland valley near relatives, where there was room to farm and for the animals to graze. Sometime around 1942 the group moved back to Sisomeder, a neighboring hamlet in the Kossoye parish community, where they owned parcels of land. In 1945 five of Melke's descendants established the hamlets of Cherema and Zinjero Wuha. This was a pleasant place with several springs, land suitable for cultivation and grazing, and a variety of indigenous trees, including the tree after which the area was named. *Kosso* trees bear a fruit used to treat a variety of ailments, particularly tapeworms.

The area had several advantages for the Melke/Gonnad descendants. Wubineh Yetemegne, Berihun Lemma, Melkamie Lemma, Tagele Wubineh, Taye Wubineh, and Assress Lemma all had land rights (*rist*) in the area. These rights did not mean that the land was legally apportioned, but individuals with familial rights could establish particular claims.

Since there was an abundance of unoccupied land, no legal or other conflicts with squatters or other claimants occurred. The Kossoye lands were also strategically located on the road recently built by the Italians, and at the juncture of paths from the lowlands. As early as 1945, elder residents recall, some of the founders saw it as a site for a future town.[16]

Not all of the 22 families in Cherema and Zinjero Wuha were kin. One original settler, Wubineh, is reported to have purchased a female slave named Habtish Yimer, most likely in the slave market in Gondar. She was said to have been from an Oromo locality in southern Ethiopia. Her purchase may have happened in the 1930s or 1940s after the passage of the 1931 Constitution that banned slavery. Wubineh treated Habtish Yimer (her name means, "May you bring good luck, including wealth and health") as a lesser wife or concubine. She bore a son, Bihonegn, and a daughter. The daughter married Mitiku, a man from the lowlands (*kolla*) where she seems to have lived. Bihonegn remained in Kossoye, openly claiming Wubineh as his father and identifying himself as half-brother of Taye and Tagele.[17]

Several other individuals born from these unions with outsiders also carried the stigma of slavery. They could attend church and community meetings, provided they paid their taxes, but typically did not marry people of Kemant ancestry, because the Kemant considered themselves to be a pure, higher race and class (*chewa*). The children of interethnic unions were also at significant economic disadvantage as they rarely inherited land rights equally with other children from Kemant wives. Thus these mixed descendants often worked as day laborers for very low wages—usually just grain—for anyone who needed help.

Within the hamlet, differences in the levels of assimilation into the Amhara culture also existed. While virtually everyone attended the Orthodox Christian Church and spoke at least some Amharic, in a few families one or both parents or grandparents still spoke Kemantney. Marriage also might bring girls from lowland areas where Kemant-ney was still spoken. Some of these individuals visited local Kemant religious sites, particularly sacred groves, where Kemant ancestors had been buried, and sacrifices were made to ensure rain and harvest.

At the edge of the neighborhood, across the road from Cherema and Zinjero Wuha, were other hamlets. People of the Bete Israel community lived in one settlement and made their living making and selling pottery and tools. These families moved into the area from Gondar in the 1950s. At a slightly lower altitude in the east near the Tsion Mariam church lived a substantial Amhara population that had probably been in the area for several hundred years. Their lands were considered the most fertile in the Kossoye region. The largest Kemant hamlets were south-east of the highway, in Medhane Alem.

Attendance at the parish churches reflected these various ethnic and religious allegiances. Tsion Mariam had an exclusively Amhara congregation and was farthest from the Kemant hamlets. Although Medhane Alem church was located in a Kemant neighborhood, it also drew Kemant people who traveled considerable distances to worship there. Bata Mariam church, located closest to the road and between the three groups, had a mix of Amhara and Kemant congregants, although the Amhara were historically in the leadership positions as head priests. The Bete Israel had their own house of worship and maintained strong group boundaries. They traded pottery and tools for cereals and animals. They would occasionally drink beer with Kemant and Amhara, but they ate separately, and their children almost never intermarried.

Religious and ethnic boundaries were reinforced in patterns of spousal selection. Parents sought marriage partners for their children from their own ethnic groups, generally from locations outside the area. In 1964, 55% of the wives came from the lowlands (*kolla*), 13.5% from Wallage, 4.5% from Wolleka, 4.5% from Fenter. Two spouses were identified as coming from Janifenkera and Kerker, places well known for Kemant communities and history.[18] Marriage was a source of mobility, particularly for girls who, as a rule, moved away from their families.

While marriage was one way to maintain ethnic boundaries, it also served as a way to bridge them. Thus while Bete Israel members almost never married Kemant or Amhara members, and while Kemant members generally married other Kemant, occasionally there were marriages between the Kemant and Amhara. At least by the nineteenth century marriage to Amhara families seems to have been an avenue for individuals from Kemant communities to gain social and economic advantages they would not have had as members of a minority group.

Traditional Education

For hundreds of years the primary avenue for Kemant assimilation into the dominant Amhara culture was conversion to Christianity. The Ethiopian Orthodox Church had a tradition of writing that required priests and deacons to be educated. For most deacons and minor priests, education came through rote learning of Geez script in a local parish church school. A few privileged local priests such as Taye Wubineh's oldest son, Sisay, traveled to Gojjam to learn *kene* (religious poetry) at a monastery. In Kossoye in 1963, all the local educational opportunities came through the church, but these were not open to even 10% of the population. There were no literate adults in Cherema or Zinjero Wuha, excepting the priests. Moreover, most peasants saw little value in education. As Tadelle Mengesha put it, "Villagers value their cattle more than their child's education, so it is quite obvious that a farmer should have at least one child to look after cattle, although this is not the case with poor farmers who have no cattle at all."[19]

In 1964 parents who wished to educate their children had two options. The first and closest was the church school in Medhane Alem, about a mile from Cherema and Zinjero Wuha. In 1964 three children from Kossoye went to this school for instruction from a Tigrayan priest, Kes Genet. The cost was 50 Ethiopian *birr* annually, in addition to the one *kuna* of grain (about 10 kilos) all farmers (including those who farm for others) were required to give to the church. Another option was the government school in Ambaghiorgis, about eight kilometers away. The costs associated with sending a child to this school were primarily logistical—travel, food, and lodging. Lodging involved staying with a relative, if one had family in town. Only one family in Cherema and Zinjero Wuha chose this route. Tadelle concluded, "Thus, only those people who have relatives and who are also rich can send their children to government schools."[20]

Children were considered educable between the ages of 6 and 14. Parents preferred to send the younger children, in part because of the lesser value of their labor. In 1964 Tadelle reported that of 67 children in the village, only 4 were in school.

Table 2.2: School Age Children in Kossoye, 1964

	Male	Female	Totals
Pre-school (1-5 years)	16	12	28
School age (6-14)	10	20	30
Total	26	32	58

But there was a movement in the area to start a government school "like the ones in Ambaghiorghis and Gondar." Tadelle reported that the decision to build a local school was made in 1961 at a *senbete* meeting. "Practically all the people at Cherema and Zenjiro Wuha [would] like to have a new government school. There was no one who did not see the need for the school."[21] Cherema was chosen as the site for a new school building for a number of reasons, including that it was on the main road.

At first Kes Eshete Bogale was given the responsibility for negotiating permission from government officials in Ambaghiorgis to build the school. This made sense, because as the *atbia dagna* and a priest, he was the most influential and formal local leader. But, for a number of reasons, action on the school was delayed. Cost was one concern, especially for poor farmers already burdened by the taxes to the government and the church. Given the fluctuations in their incomes, in part a result of variations in climate and pest infestations, they often were on the margins of existence, not inclined to obligate themselves to new fixed costs. Another concern was that the school would make the village more attractive to outsiders. One commonly expressed fear was that thieves would arrive to disrupt the village. While this was said to be fear-mongering on the part of lazy people, villagers were concerned about extra social burdens. As Tadelle explained, "Cherema is a meeting spot for traders from the lowlands, and people who miss buses en route to Gondar spend the night here. As it is the chosen site for the school, the new building meant more burden for residents. In the words of one woman, 'if the school is to be built, there are relatives around who will have their children stay at Cherema for their schooling. We will be depressed economically since help to relatives is a social obligation.'"[22]

The Subsistence Economy

Families lived in clusters of round, waddle and daub dwellings with thatched grass roofs. Most survived almost entirely without cash, growing crops and keeping cows, sheep, and goats. Surpluses from selling grain or livestock in the local markets went for taxes and goods that could only be purchased with money. Kossoyans functioned within a subsistence agricultural economy barely connected to national and international markets. Their well-being was determined primarily by weather, the soil, their labors, health, and age. Housing in Kossoye made it appear that residents shared essentially equal economic conditions. Most residents had animals and several parcels of land, averaging about three hectares (approximately 7.5 acres). All except the poorest families had enough to eat, including occasional meat, vegetables, milk, and seasonal honey. Nobody had modern possessions (such as radios or telephones) or discretionary income.[23]

Land was the foundation for the agricultural economy and wealth in rural Ethiopia. Alemayehu Abraha wrote down several phrases repeated by Kossoyans on the subject: "Land can never be sick." "Land can never vanish like cattle and other animals." "Land is a real property which anybody can be proud of and can have confidence about his over-all socio-economic position in his community." He noted, "Kossoyans strongly disapprove or invalidate a person's wealth if his resources entirely depend upon animals."[24]

The most important social transactions—birth, marriage, death—depended on the ownership and use of land. Ownership of land was usually passed from fathers to children, male and female, although women sometimes did bequeath property to their descendants. The governing principle for dividing land between male children was equality. Inheritance came at the time of marriage and when the patriarch died.

Fathers did not always show equal regard for all their children in their inheritances. Even among brothers who inherited supposedly equal shares of land, there could be differences. Kossoyans provided several scenarios. In one, an ambitious and greedy brother might take advantage of the others by claiming the most fertile lands "so that he may have an important place in the society." While the poorer brothers may want to take the richer brother to court, the legal costs typically left them only feeling resentful. In a second scenario, laziness or diligence distinguished the brothers, making some more prosperous. In a third scenario, since all lands were not equally fertile, fate could make one brother better off than another. Alemayehu noted that Wubineh pointed out to him that the differences in wealth in Kossoye could be explained in terms of land claims made by the original settlers. Some ended up with fertile parcels and others with less productive plots.[25]

Land was also a primary criterion in marriage decisions. As Mulugeta Mengistu reported in 1964: "A poor person could get his mate from a poor family, the reason being his economical status. The same thing is true with a person from a rich family. Marriage…therefore takes place between families of equal economical resources."[26] Parents attempted to establish for their children the best economic advantage possible, based on land and livestock wealth that could be transferred from fathers to sons or daughters.

Although this was a patriarchal system, with land passed through the father to the children, a wife retained rights to the original dowry. Alemayehu noted that even if a husband "resents the quality of his wife he does not divorce her" because "if he divorces he knows what hazards and poverty he is going to confront."[27] Thus some women passed on property to children or others, if they managed through divorce and widowhood to retain control of their own assets.

This system of inheritance left women at a significant disadvantage to men. If a wife died, especially after a marriage that had lasted several years, her land usually stayed with her husband. If her husband died, a woman was likely to retain some of the wealth she brought to the marriage, but if she divorced, her father may or may not reclaim his property and give it to her. If a father died before all his female children were married, lands and livestock that might have been given as dowries were likely to be divided between sons, possibly leaving the daughters with little property.

Land was valuable because it produced edible and marketable crops. Most households grew a field of barley (*gebs*), which was made into beer (*tella*) and consumed through the year. This was a cash crop for women, and especially if they were concubines or divorcees. Those with additional fields grew other grains and pulses (*senef, telba, baqella, sindie, temenj, bozie, aja*). Each of these crops could also be converted into food, money, or tax payments.

One measure used to calculate the wealth of the richest Kossoyan was *kuna*. One *kuna* is equal to 10 kilograms. In 1965 the richest man in town grew ten *kuna* of grain per year. The average for the poor farmers was reported to be four *kuna* of grain.[28] The local priest who taught children at the Medhane Alem Church received one *madiga* of grain from each family. One *madiga* is equal to one-sixth of a *kuna*, or approximately 2 kilograms of wheat. Every family also owed the church one *kuna* of grain annually, in addition to portions collected for government taxes by the *chika shum*. Usually the *chika shum* gathered all the grain and sold it in the market so he could pay the village taxes with cash.

Another source of wealth was animals. Beasts of burden commanded the highest prices. In the 1960s mules were valued at 80 Ethiopian Birr (EB) each; Sudan donkeys (a larger variety preferred for breeding mules) at 50 EB; oxen at 40 EB; horses at 35 EB; and donkeys 22 EB.[29] Animals that provided meat, milk, and butter were also important. For obvious reasons females were more valuable: goats (20 EB for females, 7 EB for males); sheep (20 EB females, 10 EB for males); cows (60 EB). Alemayehu noted that although Kossoyans liked goat milk they did not drink it often because of concern for the welfare of the young goats. They also did not want to encourage milk drinking among unsupervised shepherd boys.[30]

Table 2.3 Animal wealth in Kossoye, 1965

Individual	SEX	Mules	Donkey	Cows	Oxen	Horses	Goats	S.Donkey	Sheep	Chickens	Value in E.B.
1.	M	0	2	10	6	4	2	1	10	0	1128.
2.	M	0	0	0	3	0	0	0	4	0	160.
3.	M	0	2	3	3	2	8	0	10	0	560.
4,	M	0	1	2	1	0	2	0	0	0	196.
5.	M	0	0	0	0	0	0	0	0	0	0.
6.	M	1	1	6	4	1	2	0	0	0	671.
7.	M	0	1	0	0	0	1	0	2	0	49.
8.	M	0	0	1	0	0	0	0	0	0	60.
9.	M	0	0	3	2	1	2	0	0	0	309.
10.	M	0	1	2	2	0	0	0	3	0	252.
11.	M	0	2	2	1	1	1	0	0	10	339
12.	M	0	0	1	2	0	0	1	0	2	141
13.	M	0	0	0	0	0	0	0	0	3	1.5
14.	M	0	1	2	2	2	0	0	10	5	396.5
15.	M	0	1	1	3	1	0	0	1	3	258.5
16.	M	0	1	1	3	1	0	0	2	3	258.5
17.	M	0	0	3	1	0	4	0	0	4	250.
18.	M	0	0	1	0	0	0	0	0	3	61.5
19.	M	0	0	2	1	0	0	0	0	1	161.
20.	M	0	2	4	4	2	1	1	15	6	724.
21.	M	0	2	4	3	0	0	0	6	5	466.
22.	M	0	0	5	1	0	0	0	0	2	341.
23.	F	0	0	2	0	2	0	0	0	0	190.
24.	F	0	1	4	1	0	1	0	1	4	321.

Source: Alemayehu Abraha, p. 12.

The problem with livestock as wealth was its vulner-ability. One hazard was predatory animals. In a three-day campaign in 1964, a sanitarian student from the college, Amare Beyene, used strychnine to poison about 30 hyenas.[31] Another hazard was theft. Villagers were ever watchful for bandits from the lowlands who would snatch animals and disappear over the escarpment. Then there was the escarpment itself. Alemayehu noted that villagers reported the loss of some 20 animals which fell over the cliff during an unspecified period of time.[32] In addition, there were many diseases, some of which could wipe out an entire herd in one or two weeks.

The Kossoyans were at first reluctant to disclose any information about their personal wealth to Alemayehu. Eventually he persuaded one elder, Berihun Lema, to be his informant about animal possession and estimated value. (See Table 2.3 for comparisons in animal wealth. The original table included names of individuals, which have been omitted here.) Although no one was willing to speak about specific landholdings, even if alluded to and generally known, Berihun claimed to be the wealthiest villager. His livestock holdings, valued at 1128 EB, included two donkeys, ten cows, six oxen, four horses, two goats, one Sudan donkey, and ten sheep. No one else had so many oxen, suggesting his relatively greater landholdings. Although Alemayehu does not specify who produced ten *kuna* of grain annually, it was probably Berihun Lema.

His brother, Melkamie Lema, was reported to be the third richest man in the village in 1965. He had 671 EB worth of livestock and was the only person in town with a mule, a major status symbol. Their cousin, Taye Wubineh, was the second richest man with livestock valued at 724 EB. Taye did not have a mule but owned a Sudan donkey and two horses, so a mule could possibly be sired in the future. Both Melkamie and Taye had four oxen, indicating that they had significant parcels of land to plow. No one else in the village had more than 500 EB worth of livestock. Seventeen of twenty-two households had oxen, indicating widespread access to land and active involvement in cultivation. Taye and Tagele's father, Wubineh, was retired and had transferred his property to his children.

The fact that Alemayehu reported a range of annual grain production between four and ten *kuna* suggests differences in land wealth. The biggest producer of wheat (at 100 kilos) probably did not have much more than twice as much land as those who produced 40 kilos. Land was usually received through dowries and inheritance in fairly small plots of one to two hectares. The third wealthiest man, for example, had eight plots of land, perhaps ten hectares (24.71 acres) in all. It is unlikely that the richest had more than 20 hectares (49 acres). Studies of agriculture in highland Ethiopia suggest that ox-plow farmers can cultivate 2.5 to 5 hectares annually.[33] Cultivating 20 hectares, even with six oxen, required supplemental labor (from sons or hired help). Farmers producing four *kuna* of wheat annually probably farmed two or three plots totaling 3-6 hectares.

The average villager owned about 300 EB of livestock. A typical holding included one or two donkeys, three cows, one or two oxen, and perhaps a horse, a few sheep or goats, and several chickens. The poorest villager, whose mother had been a slave, had no livestock. Four other individuals were credited with owning a couple chickens and perhaps a cow or sheep. None of these people had oxen, suggesting that they did not inherit land. There were also landless persons in the village.

Another source of wealth was trees. Before 1965 Kossoyans generally did not place much value in trees. There were significant stands of indigenous bushes and trees (*girar, atat, kega, getem, doqma, weira, endod, kosso*) that served many purposes.[34] The three wealthiest men (Berihun, Taye, and Melkamie) grew modest numbers of eucalyptus trees, which Emperor Menelik II brought to Ethiopia from Australia in the 1890s. In 1965 Taye had 250 trees, Berihun 143 trees, and Melkamie 106 trees. Two other individuals each owned 10 eucalyptus trees with a combined value of less than 20 EB, approximately the price of one donkey.

Children were a form of wealth (or at least labor and security). Boys worked as shepherds and helped manage livestock. Girls fetched water, took care of younger siblings, and helped around the house. Grown children, especially males, were expected to support their parents in their old age. Repeatedly echoing the teachings of the Orthodox Church, men and women would say that children were God's blessing. But about forty percent of children died before their fifth birthdays.[35] And children also presented economic liabilities, especially when families did not have enough land or food. If children went to school, they required notebooks and school fees. When children married there was the cost of dowries and setting them up with land and livestock. Wedding feasts could also be expensive, requiring the feeding and entertaining of friends and relatives.

Other measures of wealth had less utility. In housing, Alemayehu found little difference between the rich and poor. All the 24 *tukul*s had similar qualities: thatched roofs, wood and mud walls, mud floors, and no windows. It was also difficult to tell much difference in personal dress. Only one person in town, Taye, wore modern manufactured boots. All the rest wore shoes made from old tires or were barefoot.

The Natural and Spiritual Worlds

Life in Kossoye was influenced by a calendar affected by the agricultural seasons and the Church. During the dry season from October until May, most villagers lived in Kossoye. The children (mostly although not exclusively boys) watched the livestock grazing on common lands, taking care that the animals did not fall to their deaths off the escarpment or fall prey to wild animals (hyenas, large cats, baboons, wild boars, foxes). The men farmed a variety of grains and lentils (*telba, ater, baqela, temenj, sindie, bozie*). With the beginning of the rainy season in June, when it could become cold enough to die of exposure, families sometimes took their herds to the lowlands (Kentobo, Janifenkera, Merobo, and Janwara) where their cattle fattened on abundant grass and forage. At the end of the rains in September, shepherds returned with their animals to the highlands, ready for a new season of cultivation and harvests.[36]

There were many reasons for this pattern of movement between the highlands (*degga*) and the lowlands (*kolla*). The most important was that the highlands, although cold and windy during the rainy season, were generally healthier than the lowlands, where there were many febrile diseases, especially malaria. Moreover, both locations had unique security advantages. During times of political stability, the highlands were closer to the feudal governments and thus more secure from bandits. During times of political instability, as in the Italian occupation, the lowlands were more secure from soldiers who might forcibly draft the young men, rape women, steal livestock, or exact other tribute.

Moving between the highland and lowlands also offered economic and social advantages. During the rainy season livestock thrived on lowland forage, and in general the lowlands were more fertile, with two or three growing seasons instead of one. If someone were sick, the common advice from a medicine man (*tenkwai*) would be to move to the highlands for cool weather or to the lowlands for warmth. Similarly, if economic expectations were not met, perhaps because of a loss of livestock or a poor harvest, common advice was to move to another location.

The Ethiopian Orthodox Church exerted a powerful influence on daily life. Priests taught that virtually everything in the natural world is divinely inspired. Good behavior on the part of humans would be rewarded by bountiful harvests, good health, and the birth of children. Bad behavior would be punished by famine, illness, and infertility.

Holidays provided one way to show respect to the Creator and the Saints. In most months, even in the harvest season, more days were devoted to religion than to work. Alemayehu calculated that after Sundays and Saturdays, St. Michael's Day, St. Mary's Day, Baalegzabher, and other holidays only fourteen days were left for work in an average month. Some of these work days were lost for funerals, marriages, court appearances, trips to market, or sickness, reducing productive time even further. "The Kossoye people are…very religious," Alemayehu noted. "They say that every evil that occurs in nature is the result of working during holidays. They strongly believe that if they work on a holiday a strong rain may sweep away their farm areas or hail [may] destroy their crops."[37]

The sense that all natural events had divine causation diminished an appreciation of the value of individual effort and undermined the work ethic. Bad harvests, the loss of an animal, the birth or death of a child—all of these could be explained as God's will. Farmers planned and worked, some harder than others, but it was within a religious culture that constrained productivity. Alemayehu concluded that "holidays have affected the people in their economy."[38] In other words, the Orthodox religion reduced the sense that individual agency, planning, and applied effort might make a difference.

Conclusion

Characteristic of rural societies around the world, Kossoyans were reluctant to confront long-range problems with scientific and rational problem-solving. They saw all natural events—from childbirth to rains and harvests—as divinely caused. Life proceeded through the seasons. Human plans were based on tradition.

In this sense the Kossoyans' interest in improving the quality of their local beer is revealing. At that point they did not understand how to avoid diarrhea and other water-borne illnesses. The priority was, rather, the enjoyment of the *senbete* meeting, socializing with neighbors and friends, while also avoiding upsetting a larger moral order presided over by a vengeful and powerful God.

Differences in family wealth made it meaningful to speak of rich and poor, but even the wealthiest persons lived as subsistence farmers without savings for more than a few months. Wealth was not measured in money but rather in land and in commodities that could be turned into cash—crops and animals. Only a few individuals had enough money for a bus ticket, to buy shoes, or to send a child to school. The wealthiest Kossoyan owned only about 10-12 hectares of land. Divided between four or five male children, even with favorable dowries, the size of landholdings and resulting annual crop harvests was bound to diminish unless more land could be found or other kinds of economic activity could be developed.

Forty years later, in the early twenty-first century, older Kossoyans recalled that life in the 1960s was good. The wealthiest families always had enough to eat and even ate well. Poor families could rely on their relatives and neighbors. Droughts occurred from time to time, but in the highlands people had coping strategies, including moving to the lowlands.

Notes

1. Frederick C. Gamst, *The Qemant: A Pagan-Hebraic Peasantry of Ethiopia* (New York: Holt, Rinehart, and Winston, Inc., 1969).

2. Gamst, *The Qemant*, 11.

3. Taddesse Tamrat, "Processes of Ethnic Interaction and Integration in Ethiopian History: The Case of the Agaw" in *Proceedings of the Ninth International Conference on Ethiopian Studies*, Volume 6 (Moscow, 1986): 195.

4. Taddesse, "Processes of Ethnic Interaction," 205.

5. Gamst, *The Qemant*, 37.

6. Gamst, *The Qemant*, 13.

7.   Henze, *Layers of Time: A History of Ethiopia*, 111.

8   Robert O. Collins, *The Nile* (New Haven: Yale University Press, 2002), 123.

9   Gamst, *The Qemant*, 13-31.

10. Zelealem Leyew, *The Kemantney Language: A Sociolinguistic and Grammatical Study of Language Replacement* (Koln, Germany: Rudiger Koppe Verlag, 2003).

11. Zelealem, *The Kemantney Language*, chapter two.

12. Mulugeta Mengistu, "A Report on Social and Psychological Patterns of People at Cherema and Jinjero Wuha" (handscript, 1964), 3.

13. Alemayehu Abraha, "Health in the Low and High Socio-Economic Groups in Kossoye with a Brief Review on the History, Geography and Economy" (typescript, 1965), 4-5.

14. Mulugeta, 3.

15. Alemayehu, 2-5.

16. Interview 21, February 18, 1994.

17. Alemayehu, 3.

18. Mulugeta, 2-3.

19. Tadelle Mengesha, "Report on the Social and Psychological Patterns of People at Cherema and Jenjiro Wuha" (handscript, August 1964).

20. Tadelle, 1.

21. Tadelle, 4.

22. Tadelle, 6.

23   Sociologists debate definitions of subsistence economy. The phrase is used here to describe primarily self-sufficient agricultural families that would, through the 1970s and beyond, engage increasingly in selling cash crops such as eucalyptus trees. See Nicholas Abercombie, Stephen Hill, and Bryan S. Turner, *The Penguin Dictionary of Sociology*, Fourth Edition (London: Penguin Books, 2000), 350.

24. Alemayehu, 7.

25. Alemayehu, 5-8.

26. Tadelle, 2.

27. Alemayehu, 8.

28. Alemayehu, 9.

29. The exchange rate in the 1960s was fixed at an artificially high 2.20 EB per 1.00 USD, much higher than the black market rates. At present the rate floats between 9 and 10 EB per 1 USD with black market rates much closer.

30. Alemayehu, 10.

31. Amare Beyene, "Hyena Control at Kossoye Village" (typescript, May 28, 1964).

32. Alemayehu, 10.

33. James C. McCann, *People of the Plow: An Agricultural History of Ethiopia, 1800-1990* (Madison: The University of Wisconsin Press, 1995), 47.

34. Alemayehu, 13. The fruit of the bush *endod* is valuable because of its soap-like qualities.

35. Few accurate infant and child mortality rates were available in the 1960s. Infant mortality rates ranged from 83 (in Metu) to 196 per 1000 live births (in Sodu) as baseline figures in Dirk Spruyt et. al., "Demonstration & Evaluation Project Ethiopian Health Center Program," *Ethiopian Medical Journal*, 1967, vol. 5, no. 3: 35-36. Other studies by Assefa Hailemariam and Helmut Kloos showed 151 IMR in 1970, "Population," in *The Ecology of Health and Disease in Ethiopia*, ed. by Kloos and Zein (Boulder: Westview Press, 1993), 59. Mortality rates for all children under five were estimated to be in the range of 400 per 1000 live births, i.e. 40% of children died before reaching their fifth year.

36. Alemayehu, 5.

37. Alemayehu, 9.

38 Alemayehu, 9.

1960s: View over the escarpment from Kossoye.

The late feudal order in Gondar: Colonel
Tamirat Yigezu (the Governor), Abuna Petros
(Archbishop of the Orthodox Church), the
military, and regional officials.

1960s: Taye Wubineh and family.

1960s: Berihun Lemma, the richest farmer in
the two hamlets.

1965: Local dignitaries and military officials, many armed with rifles, posing in front of Medhane Alem Church.

1965: The parish community, dedicating a new roof for Medhane Alem Church.

1966: Taye's brother, Tagele Wubineh, with family. The grandparents, Wubineh and Etenesh, are at the far right.

CHAPTER THREE

THE EMPEROR AND THE *CHIKA SHUM*

❖ ❖ ❖

Nineteen sixty-five was an eventful year in Kossoye. In February, Haile Sellassie and Queen Elizabeth II visited the village, staying the night in a camp erected on the outskirts of Cherema and Zinjero Wuha. It is reported that as they looked out over the escarpment toward Sudan—land through which Ethiopian and British soldiers traveled in 1941, on their way to liberating Gondar—the Emperor granted the Queen all the land she could see. The story of the Emperor's generosity, whether true or not, reflects the theory of the Emperor's absolute authority.

Remarkably, Haile Sellassie's retinue chose to camp that day in the Kossoye parish community rather than stay in the provincial capital. Gondar had castles, the Public Health College, and beautiful homes and buildings. Indeed, at some point in the 1950s Haile Sellassie is reported to have remarked that he wished that Gondar's Art Deco style bank and post office, built by the Italians, could be moved to Addis Ababa, 700 kilometers south. Gondar was also the home of the provincial governor, married to one of the Emperor's granddaughters.

In the city of Gondar the entire population of 30,000 people mobilized for the welcoming ceremonies. Individuals with private cars drove to the airport to form a caravan. The Ethiopian and British royal parties arrived in separate Douglas DC3 airplanes and then traveled by car into the city, followed by the procession. The streets were lined with thousands of people and adorned with banners, translated into English by American Peace Corps teachers:

> "Oh Queen! This is Gondar, the home of learning and religious poetry."
> "Our longing was not in vain! We are happy, for we see Elizabeth because of Haile Sellassie."
> "King and Queen! Enter with joy, for this is the entrance to Gondar."
> "The ancient capital, Gondar, by the visit of HM Queen Elizabeth and Prince Philip, Duke of Edinburgh, receives guests to her historic honor."
> "Welcome to their two majesties. We rejoice with you."
> "The two majesties are visiting the land cleaned and freed   by their patriots' blood."[1]

The receiving ceremony was held in the piazza, in front of the palace compound built by King Fasiledes and his dynasty from the 1630s into the late 19th century.

In Kossoye the procession was greeted by hundreds of men on brightly decorated horses. In honor of the occasion the horsemen put on a dazzling display of equestrian skill. Then the royal parties proceeded to the very edge of the escarpment where government workers had erected a tent city that included bathrooms with running water and gold faucets. The BBC explained, "Ethiopians have had experience in luxury camping ever since the time of the Queen of Sheba. Their kings used to have moveable capitals until the Gondar time, and this tent camp was a model of efficient, comfortable planning."[2]

The Emperor's attention was prized wherever he traveled. On this occasion both the College and the parish community were granted brief audiences. In recollections of the event the villagers disagreed on whether he shook any of their hands —a familiarity which seems unlikely, given the great social distance between the Emperor and even a *chika shum*. But there is no disagreement that one of Haile Sellassie's aides distributed currency notes (*birr*) to each of the sixty or so heads of families.

Later some villagers wondered why the Emperor visited Kossoye. Some thought he had come for reasons associated with the College. There is no evidence about the decision-making process. It seems that the Emperor's planners chose the site for the view and the fact that it was surrounded by friendly subjects.

The Emperor's visit came at a propitious time in Kossoye's history. Taye Wubineh, a farmer and the local *chika shum*, had embarked on a series of innovations. In the summer of 1964 he had asked a relative who worked in Addis Ababa to give a public talk in Kossoye about modernization. In October 1964 Taye built the first modern rectangular house with windows and a corrugated metal roof. In the fall of 1965 he hired the first teacher for the government school that he helped build. He also planted 6,000 eucalyptus trees, the first tree farm in the area.

Why did all this activity happen in 1964 and 1965, rather than at some other time? How did a rural farmer who could neither read nor write come to visualize and desire major changes for himself, his family, and his social and physical environment? Sources of outside stimulation included the Public Health College, the Emperor, and conversations with Alemayehu Abraha and Dennis Carlson. The argument advanced in this chapter is that while outside influences mattered, much of Taye's motivation to seize opportunities for change came from his parents and the local environment.

The *Chika Shum*

When he first arrived in Kossoye, Dennis Carlson sought to identify the local leaders. Taye acted the part by welcoming the visitors and presenting himself as community spokesman. In discussions with the students, Carlson predicted, based on Taye's outgoing personality, that he would be the innovator. Subsequently one health officer student, Alemayehu Abraha, "decided to trace [Taye's] life history so that I may find out some elements which helped him to achieve such a personality. The life history can be a good data in relating innovation, health and economy."[3]

Alemayehu found that Taye was born to a family that was making its way, over two or three generations, into the local Amhara elite. His father, Wubineh Yetemegn, was born in Ambaras in the late 1880s. The family oral history says that Wubineh's grandfather was among the first in the family to convert, in the late nineteenth century, from the Kemant religion to the Ethiopian Orthodox Church.

Wubineh lived his life in relatively prosperous circumstances. His grandson recalled that he had ten hectares of land, six oxen, and many cattle.[4] He served for six years as *chika shum* in the Ambaras area where he owned land and farmed. He had two sons and five daughters. In addition, Wubineh had a second family with his concubine, Habtish Yimer, who bore him two more children. Her son, Bihonegn, lived in Cherema. At the time of the first college census in 1965, Wubineh lived in Kossoye with his wife, Etanat Desta, and two daughters (Kebebush and Wagaw), who had married local men. Habtish Yimer and her children also lived nearby.

Wubineh had won local acclaim after the Italian occupation when he and Kes Bogale (Kes Eshete's father) successfully brought the Ark replica (*tabot*) back to Bata Mariam church from the lowland church in Belessa, where it had been taken for safekeeping, during the Italian occupation.[5] After the war the Bata priests were reluctant to reestablish the church without their old *tabot*. After Wubineh and Kes Bogale succeeded in returning the *tabot*, they received approval from church authorities to build another church that was clearly in Kemant territory. Thus in 1945 or 1946 a new church was constructed about a mile from Cherema and the road. It was named Medhane Alem (Savior of the World). The residents say that Haile Sellassie built the new church, meaning the building was constructed during his reign.

Taye spent his childhood in the 1920s on his father's lands at the edge of the escarpment in Ambaras, 5 kilometers northeast of Kossoye on the road to Ambaghiorgis. From age six to fifteen he shepherded his father's cattle. He believed he was favored by his father because of his work ethic. He found good pasture for the livestock and kept them away from danger. He reported that he used his father's trousers as a pillow and usually slept with him. As an adult, reflecting on his youth, Taye felt he was the favorite child. Taye told Alemayehu that even as adults his siblings remained jealous of him.[6]

Young Taye experienced advantages that indicated his father's affection. In 1928 at the age of ten he made his first trip to the large regional market in Gondar, helping his parents manage the donkeys carrying bags of grain and other goods. These trips to Gondar may have helped his father establish connections that resulted in a beneficial marriage agreement. In 1938, at the age of 20, Taye was married to a girl from a Gondar family. The dowry included five cows and title to five pieces of land. His father also gave the young couple his best animals and pieces of land. Young Taye had an unusually prosperous start as a farmer.

The Italian occupation, which began in 1936, caused many troubles for Taye. In 1938, soon after his marriage, the entire extended family fled the highlands to Gundi Chugie Mariam in the deep valley below their home in Ambaras. In the lowlands they had many relatives and access to land for farming and grazing. Tragically, in 1940 Taye's young wife died after a five-day fever, leaving him with two young daughters, one who also died. Later he married a fifteen-year-old girl from the lowlands. Semu Yilma's dowry included four cows and seven or eight pieces of land.[7] By his early 20s, combined with the lands and cows he retained from his first wife, and the lands and herds he received from his father and second wife, Taye had substantial wealth in land and livestock. (It appears that two or three pieces of land were returned to his first wife's family, since the couple had only been married two years.)

After the Italians were driven out of Ethiopia in 1941, the extended family returned to the highlands but not to Ambaras. Their first move was to one of the hamlets in the Kossoye parish, Sisomeder, where they had relatives and land rights (*rist*). In 1945 Taye moved again, this time to Cherema and Zinjero Wuha. Accompanying him were his father, his brother Tagele, and three cousins, Berihun Lemma, Melkamie Lemma, and Assress Lemma.

Cherema and Zinjero Wuha were considered prime locations since they were at the conjunction of the new highway and a well-traveled pathway between the lowlands and highlands. Some of the early settlers, including Taye, are reported to have dreamed that their community would become a town, perhaps like nearby Ambaghiorgis and Gondar. Taye surely recognized the greater opportunities for commerce and wealth in urban settings.

Taye lived with his family in Cherema for several years, and then in the early 1950s moved back to Ambaras where he attained the position as *chika shum*. In the *chika shum* role he collected taxes and represented the community in court and at other official government affairs. This involved travel to Ambaghiorgis and Gondar. In 1952, at the age of 34, he made his first trip to Addis Ababa, traveling by bus through Tigray and Wello. Subsequently he made several other visits to Addis Ababa, in his official capacity as a *chika shum*. A few years later he moved back to Cherema because his animals were not doing well in Ambaras. One of Taye's greatest successes in the *chika shum* role was when he led a posse to the Tekaze River valley to arrest thieves. For this accomplishment he was named *shambel*, meaning that he supervised 15 other *chika shums*.[8]

By 1964, when Alemayehu Abraha began his research in Kossoye, Taye had become the second wealthiest person in Cherema and Zinjero Wuha. Wealth fluctuated, especially as children were married and given land and cattle. In 1965 Alemayehu learned that Taye owned 14 pieces of land, some located in the lowlands, some around Kossoye, and some in Ambaras. He also had a growing livestock herd of three donkeys, five cows, six oxen, four horses, two goats, twenty sheep, and ten chickens. During the worst harvests he collected ten *kuna* (100 kilos) of wheat; with good weather, he collected more.[9]

Well before the 1960s Taye was an enterprising and hardworking person. Alemayehu noted that he had been ambitious since his childhood. Because he did not have opportunity to go to school—a source of acute personal embarrassment—Taye devoted himself to becoming a rich farmer and *chika shum*. These accomplishments brought him respect and prestige in the community. They probably also gave him the assurance to try new ideas. Alemayehu noted that this fit Bast F. Hoselitz's argument about the defining qualities of innovators: "the one who for some reason espouses a new idea and devotes himself energetically to selling it to his society."[10] Alemayehu was especially impressed by the attention Taye gave his children. Every morning before they went to school, he supervised them as they washed their faces. Before they went to bed, he made sure they washed their feet and legs. He also provided each with two changes of clothing, one for daily wear and the other for special occasions.

Alemayehu described his relationship with Taye in some detail in his 1965 paper. "When I was making the study of health and wealth in 1964, I was visiting every house interviewing people and looking at the property of every person in the community. In the meantime I came in contact with Ato Taye. Taye's personality impressed me very much [Alemayehu wrote]. He is one of the richest men in the community, he had an overcoat, modern shoes, neat clothes, and modern equipments were available in his home. Moreover, he toiled and toiled all the time and was never seen in the hamlet except on holidays, had many eucalyptus trees, but he was never satisfied with them and wanted to increase his property through hard work."[11]

Trips to Addis Ababa seem to have influenced Taye's vision for his community. "When Ato Taye returned from Addis Ababa [wrote Alemayehu after a trip in 1964] his mind was concentrated with digested and undigested ideas, with solvable and unsolvable problems…. He thought that Cherema could be a town and houses could be built with corrugated iron sheets, schools could be constructed, a market could be established, a grinding mill could be installed, and other enterprises could prevail."[12] The grinding mill, he thought, could be purchased through a common fund (which Alemayehu described as a "trade union"), subscribed to by all the villagers.

Taye told Alemayehu that he would like to "eat small and live in Addis Ababa." He was especially amazed at the tall buildings, the busy traffic, and the many shops. But he became depressed when he realized that nearly everything that happened in government offices was "written on paper."[13] Unable to read or write, he had a severe handicap. In 1964 he sent his oldest son, Sisay, for education in monasteries located in Gondar and Gojjam. Convinced that all his children needed education, Taye resolved to build a government school in Kossoye.

His neighbors were not receptive to this plan. As Alemayehu put it, "The idea of Ato Taye has not crystallized in the minds of the people." The villagers had three concerns: first, that more thieves would come into the area; second, that they would have more houseguests from the lowlands; and finally, that powerful persons from outside of Kossoye would come into the area and "snatch their land." Taye was acutely disappointed. He told Alemayehu that his friend Melkamie, one of the three wealthiest men in Cherema and Zingero Wuha, opposed his plans because he had not traveled to the city and feared that if his children went to school they would not take care of his animals.[14]

During the rainy season of 1965 (June to September), Ferede Baynesagn, one of Taye's friends in Addis Ababa, visited Kossoye. This friend, Taye thought, might be able to convince villagers of the need for modernization. Ferede was a relative of the Cherema and Zinjero Wuha clan and had grown up in the area. Somehow he learned to read and write Amharic and to speak English. Then he found work in Addis Ababa, for a time in a United States Embassy position. Ferede was also an entrepreneur. Whenever Taye went to the big city, he visited Ferede and sought his advice. Ferede's visit to him in Kossoye was a favor.

Taye arranged for Ferede Baynesagn to talk to the community about modernizing. Ferede advised people to plant eucalyptus trees as a cash crop, to educate their children, and to "contribute money to do some beneficial things to themselves like, perhaps, buying a grinding mill." The Kossoyans listened but did not act. Alemayehu concluded: "So, unless the person who advises them is present with them until they accomplish what they have accepted, everything cannot be fulfilled."[15]

Taye was the exception. He made a partnership with Ferede to start a eucalyptus plantation with 6,000 seedlings. At nearly the same time, Taye began building the first modern rectangular home. The new house had a corrugated metal roof, a sleeping room with a window, and floors and walls plastered with a mud/dung mixture. It also had a kerosene lamp and a picture of Crown Prince Phillip, no doubt collected at the time of the royal visit in February 1965.

Taye began building the government school during the rainy season of 1965. Ferede provided money for nails and corrugated metal sheets for the roof. Taye gathered stone and eucalyptus trees. Some villagers helped. In October 1965 when a new group of college students came to Kossoye, Taye invited them to join him, barefoot, in the pit of gooey *chika* to help mix the mud and straw.

The first teacher employed at the school in September 1965 was a Tigrayan priest from Medhane Alem Church, Kes Genet Alemayehu. Until a government teacher was assigned, Kes Genet was paid by the students' families. The curriculum was similar to that of the church school: students learned the alphabet (*fidel*), reading, and writing, through rote repetition. Children from Cherema, Zinjero Wuha, Medhane Alem, and surrounding hamlets in the Kossoye parish community were the first students, but before long, as predicted, people in the lowlands began sending their children on the half-day hike up the escarpment to attend the new school. Seventy-four students were enrolled in the first year. Two-thirds were girls, a marked contrast to urban schools where boys made up the majority, as farmers preferred that their sons stay home to help with herding and cultivation.

Negative attitudes towards the school continued after classes had begun. Some community elders, particularly Berihun Lemma, feared that they would be required to provide shelter and food for relatives' children. His younger brother, Melkamie, who lived next door, sided with him and vowed he would never allow his children to attend. In September 1966, a few weeks after the school reopened for the second year, a whooping cough epidemic struck the community. Three children died, including one of Berihun's daughters. Some residents believed children from the lowlands brought the disease to Kossoye. Berihun demanded that the school be permanently closed to prevent introduction of other diseases.

By the end of the school year in 1967, one hundred seventeen pupils, perhaps a quarter of the school-age children in the community, were enrolled and the ratio of females to males had become equal. Taye had secured two male teachers from the Ministry of Education to teach the standard first and second grade government curriculum. A school director/teacher had been appointed as a third staff member, and a large piece of land was set aside for the school near the escarpment where Emperor Haile Sellassie had hosted Queen Elizabeth and Prince Phillip. Several new classrooms were constructed on the new site by community members in collaboration with the Ministry of Education.

While the school was one example of innovation, Taye and Ferede's eucalyptus plantation was another. In 1964 Taye was not an active tree planter. When Alemayehu conducted his study of health and economy, Berihun had 143 trees, half less than ten centimeters (four inches) in circumference, indicating recent planting. His brother Melkamie had 106 trees. Taye had approximately 250 trees.

By the end of 1965 the idea of tree planting had taken hold. Ferede convinced Taye that excellent profits could be realized by planting eucalyptus seedlings on a large scale and selling them to truckers who would transport them to the markets of Gondar, Mekelle, and Asmara. Ferede obtained 6,000 young plants and brought them to Kossoye. Taye planted them in a field where there was ample water. The next year Taye began collecting eucalyptus seeds gathered at the Medhane Alem Church grounds. He planted them in beds below the protected spring where overflow water ran down the steep slope. Soon fourteen neighbors in Cherema and three from nearby hamlets imitated him. Taye also sowed several garden plots of carrots and green leafy vegetables (later abandoned because of enthusiasm for eucalyptus planting).

One day when college students were working in the village, Berihun asked Dennis Carlson for eucalyptus seedlings. Taye overheard the request and scolded Berihun, asking why he couldn't get seeds from the churchyard. Berihun responded that he did not have children who could climb up into the trees. "At that point Taye told Berihun that he was lazy" and told him that he had found the seeds under the trees in the churchyard.[16] Subsequently Berihun became an enthusiastic tree farmer.

Eucalyptus trees grow quickly and are marketable within five years. By 1970 Taye and Ferede were selling several hundred trees a year to truckers who hauled them to urban markets. Such profit with relatively little labor was so attractive that eucalyptus tree farming spread over the high plateau, especially between Ambaghiorgis and Gondar. From 1970 to 1974 extensive eucalyptus plantings appeared on property controlled by the Medhane Alem Church, on the new school compound, and on nearly all homesteads in Cherema and Zinjero Wuha. By 1974 thirty-three householders in Cherema and Zinjero Wuha had young trees growing below the spring. Kes Gennet planted over 1000 eucalyptus near his home. Alemu Lemma had 215 trees, Asress Lemma had 175, and Mengistu Lemma 160 trees.[17]

Cash from the eucalyptus harvests financed several projects. New classrooms were added to the school. Berihun and Kes Eshete built rectangular homes with corrugated metal roofs and windows. Alemayehu noted, "Although Ato Berihun is rigid and static, ultimately Ato Taye stimulated him to plan."[18]

Conclusion

Why did this illiterate farmer have such an impact on his community? In 1964 and 1965, Dennis Carlson was talking to David C. Korten and Frances Korten, who were teaching in the new Business School of Haile Sellassie I University in Addis Ababa. They introduced him to possible applications of Thematic Apperception Tests (TAT) and the works of

David McClelland, who would later visit Ethiopia to study the impact of Peace Corps volunteers on development.[19] In addition to the work by Aleymayehu Abraha, several college students and faculty members adopted a set of TAT drawings, based on peasant life in Ethiopia, as a method to examine attitude differences among the Kossoyans.

The tests revealed the power of tradition among the local people. One individual saw slaves in the drawing of farmers selling sheep in the market, a perception that alerted Carlson to a history of slavery in the village. Others saw a birthing scene as a time of joy, rather than an increasing burden.[20] Taye's interpretations included more modern possibilities, fitting the "N" personality that David McClelland described in *The Achieving Society*, based upon his case studies from around the developing world. Typically "N" personalities are comparatively well off but not the wealthiest when compared to their neighbors, and so are inclined to some risk-taking to improve their positions. They treat their children well. They have good relationships with their parents. In sum, they tend to be the recipients of a combination of nurture and stimulation that creates an appetite for accomplishment.

The story of the Emperor and the *chika shum*'s meeting in the countryside north of Gondar provides insight into possibilities for innovation in the 1960s. Haile Sellassie was an absolutist monarch seeking to modernize his country by creating a new educated middle class while also balancing the interests of a land-holding aristocracy with those of a vast peasant class. Taye, in his capacity as a local leader, supported the Emperor and did his best to represent his neighbors' interests. But he also wanted improved housing, cash crops, and hoped that at least some of his children would be able to join the new middle class.

In noting the importance of local, lesser nobles in Ethiopian modernization, Donald N. Levine wrote: "Short of a brutally totalitarian program that is willing to ignore the sentiments of the mass of tradition-directed peasantry, and suffer the consequences, no dynamic program of agricultural and social development can take place in Abyssinian areas that does not enlist the active cooperation of the local *balabbat* and *shum*."[21] In 1965 in Kossoye it seemed that the Emperor and the *chika shum's* interests were compatible. Both envisioned a national culture based upon the Ethiopian Orthodox Church and Amharic as the official language. Taye had enough faith in the system that he traveled to Addis Ababa when he was frustrated by the district government in Ambaghiorgis or the provincial government in Gondar. He made specific requests for teachers and books and succeeded in making the government work for his community. He had significant achievements in Haile Sellassie's Ethiopia.

In retrospect, it is not clear that Taye's interests were well represented by Haile Sellassie's modernization policies. In the Emperor's plan the aristocrats with landholdings in the hundreds and thousands of hectares were the leaders in the development of commercial agriculture, which would then lead to investment in industry. Some so-called "rich peasants" like Taye, who had 10-15 hectares of land, may have felt included in this plan. But within the historian John Iliffe's framework, all of the Kossoyans were poor—subject to the vicissitudes of war, famine, injury, and disease that created episodes of extreme poverty.[22] Taye's father Wubineh remembered a time of the Great Famine in the 1890s. Taye would live to tell of the dark days of the Derg, in the 1970s and 1980s, when he would wait in line for food in Ambaghiorgis.

Utlimately, Taye's vision of a modern village or town, even if based in agriculture and in feudal traditions, had radical implications. His hopes for educating all his children were only partially realized. All of his six sons had some education, while none of his three daughters completed any schooling.[23] But the government school that he was instrumental in founding would become a transformative institution in Kossoye. Young children and their mothers would move to Kossoye because of the school. Graduates would go on to high school, college, and overseas opportunities. Teachers with government salaries would settle in town, bringing along modern, urban ideas and practices. The school prepared the way for the village to become a modern town.

Notes

1. Letter from Louise F. Carlson to Elsie and Louis Fiscus, February 12, 1965.

2. As cited in Louise F. Carlson letter, February 12, 1965.

3. Alemayehu Abraha, "A Case Study on the Relationship of Innovation, Health, and Economy in a Traditional Family" (Typescript, 1965).

4. Interview 28, February 21, 1994.

5. Interview 73, February 5, 2006.

6. Alemayehu, "A Case Study," 4.

7. Alemayehu, "A Case Study," 7.

8. Interview 73, February 15, 2006.

9. Alemayehu, "A Case Study," 8.

10. Alemayehu, "A Case Study," 17.

11. Alemayehu, "A Case Study," 17.

12. Alemayehu, "A Case Study," 5.

13. Alemayehu, "A Case Study," 16.

14. Alemayehu, "A Case Study," 14.

15. Alemayehu, "A Case Study," 16.

16. Alemayehu, "A Case Study," 18.

17. Dr. Tesfaye Teshome, a research scientist in forestry, has challenged the thesis that eucalyptus tree planting has a negative ecological impact in Ethiopia by reviewing economic, biologic and management issues. He cites Davison (1973) in asserting that eucalyptus is one of the more efficient users of water as compared to other com-

mercial crops in Ethiopia such as cotton, field pea, coffee, banana, soy bean, potato, maize and sorghum. He argues that without the 90% of eucalyptus marketed as fuel Ethiopia would be in desperate straits for firewood and construction poles. He concludes that the economic return on eucalyptus cultivation is one of the highest in the Ethiopian ecosystem. He states that "there are not profound reasons not to continue or to discourage eucalyptus planting in Ethiopia." See Tesfaye Teshome, PhD, "Is Eucalyptus Ecologically Hazardous Tree Species," Wondo Genet College of Forestry, Debub University, Awassa, Ethiopia, Ethiopian Tree Fund Foundation. Retrieved at http.www.ettf.org on December 10, 2006.

18. Alemayehu, "A Case Study," 15.

19. David McClelland, *The Achieving Society* (New York: D. Van Nosstrand Company, Inc. 1961).

20. Dennis Carlson asked the artist to redraw the family scene in which a baby had just been born and in which everyone in the drawing had a neutral expression. The artist could not grasp the notion that facial expressions could be "neutral" in affect. As re-drawings continued, the quality of drawing became remarkably poorer. The request for a neutral attitude toward childbirth was clearly countercultural.

21. Donald N. Levine, *Wax and Gold: Tradition and Innovation in Ethiopian Culture* (Chicago: University of Chicago, 1965, 1972), 180-181.

22. John Illife, *Poverty in Africa: A History* (Cambridge: Cambridge University Press, 1987), chapters one and two.

23. The oldest son completed the nine years of monastery education required for the priesthood. One of the youngest twin sons completed 12th grade and the other 6th grade. The other sons seem to have ended their education somewhere in earlier grades.

1965: The royal motorcade in front of the castle compound in downtown Gondar.

1965: Haile Sellassie with grandson, at the campground in Kossoye.

1965: Horsemen prepare for a tournament of traditional games in front of the royal encampment.

1965: The royal encampment, at the edge of the escarpment.

1965: Entrance to the campground for Haile Sellassie and Queen Elizabeth II.

1964?: Ato Taye, the local Chika Shum, at the protected spring. This is a great source of joy for the whole community and affirms Taye's leadership.

1965: Following Taye's example, Berayhun builds the second modern, rectangular house with windows and metal roof.

1965: Dennis Carlson with Ferede, Kes Genet, and the first-year students at the Kossoye elementary school.

1965: Students and faculty from the Haile Sellassie I College of Public Health.

1966: Sisay Taye, Ferede Beynasagn, Asefa Taye, Taye Wubineh, and Getahoun Mulat at the wedding of three of Taye's children.

1966: Andrew Carlson (age 10), dressed in his Sunday best, playing the drum at the wedding for Taye's two sons and daughter.

CHAPTER FOUR

HEALTH TRANSITION

❖ ❖ ❖

Secular education supported by the government was beginning to expand by the 1960s, but were comparable changes taking place in health and agriculture? Did Ethiopian parents see the future for their children and themselves becoming more secure? Could they count on healthier, longer lives? In other words, had the "health transition" already begun?

Simon Kuznets wrote that rapid population growth began in the 1920s and 1930s in many low-income countries where modern curative and preventive health services were spreading. Immunization programs and improved clinical services resulted in lowered death rates and longer lives for those who survived early childhood.[1] This "death control" contributed directly to steady and rapid population growth. Thomas McKeown attributed population expansion primarily to improved food production and distribution,[2] but others like Nevin Scrimshaw and Carl E. Taylor argued that the constant synergy between infectious diseases and nutritional status was more significant.[3]

Infectious diseases and nutritional disorders have been heavy burdens for Ethiopian populations throughout history. Smallpox, malaria, syphilis, typhus, cholera, and trachoma were often reported in historical accounts.[4] Drought, famine and nutritional disorders appear frequently in Ethiopian court chronicles and narratives by foreign observers.[5] Visiting medical practitioners wrote about their efforts with the health problems of rulers and their immediate court members, though sometimes they treated commoners as well.[6] The new knowledge and technologies brought by foreigners often produced dramatic results and achieved wide acclaim. How far these health improvements spread is unknown. It seems unlikely that impact on morbidity and mortality extended much beyond residents in the imperial palace and privileged members of the imperial court.

European influences were present in Ethiopia beginning in the 16th century. A barber-surgeon, Joao Bermudes, was part of the Portuguese Embassy in 1520 and made such a positive impact that Emperor Lebna Dengel wrote the following year to the King of Portugal to send a number of physicians, surgeons, and "men who make medicines." Bermudes was valued so highly that he was not allowed to leave the country when his countrymen did in 1526, but had to stay and continue practicing medicine until 1535.[7] A century later, in 1636, a German Lutheran missionary set up a clinic in the new city of Gondar with the "favor" of Emperor Fasilides.[8] In the 17th century Emperor Iyasu sent an agent to Egypt to get medical help for his son's severe skin ailment.[9]

Probably the most widely known foreign practitioner of this period was the Scot, James Bruce, who arrived in Gondar in 1770 and stayed several years. Though not trained formally as a physician, he was knowledgeable in medicine and treated thousands of people for malaria, syphilis, smallpox, and other medical complaints. He also was concerned about preventing diseases, especially malaria, for which he promoted prophylactic use of quinine in unrefined cinchona bark form. While consulting at the royal household in Gondar at the time of a smallpox outbreak, he insisted that getting more ventilation into living spaces was important. Bruce traveled extensively around Lake Tana, treating many sick commoners wherever he went.[10]

More medical visitors arrived in the 19th century with governmental and religious missions. A significant part of the motivation behind these missions arose from the intense competition among European countries to build and expand colonial empires: the "Scramble for Africa."[11] French and British scientific delegations were sent in mid-century to investigate health conditions and treat patients.[12] In the 1880s the Italians dispatched a medical mission as part of efforts to establish colonies in Africa.[13] Following the Ethio-Italian war of 1895-96, the Russian government sponsored a Red Cross mission.[14] Among the staff was a Russian medical student who wrote the first modern medical text in Amharic that addressed common illnesses and injuries found in Ethiopia.[15] Religious missions from Italy, Germany, and other European countries also sent occasional medical representatives.[16]

Emperors Tewodoros, Yohannes, and Menelik maintained strong support of health activities. Variolation was frequently used to prevent smallpox.[17] As smallpox vaccines became available, they were included in official programs. Emperors Yohannes and Menelik and top government officials were vaccinated in public settings using the new methods to publicize and promote widespread use. At the turn of the 20th century, Menelik repeatedly ordered the population to be vaccinated for smallpox.[18]

Many other modern health care advances took place under Menelik's leadership in the late 19th and early 20th century. The number of government and private pharmacies increased rapidly, especially in Addis Ababa, as importation of modern drugs rose exponentially.[19] Menelik arranged for water to be piped into his palace in 1894. The first leprosarium was established in 1901 and several hospitals were built in Addis, starting with Menelik II Hospital in 1909.[20] The regent Taferi Makonnen, crowned Emperor Haile Sellassie I in 1930, actively promoted modern medicine and public health during his long reign. He added hospitals in Addis Ababa and built institutions in the provinces during the

1920s and 1930s. A vaccine institute with a 20-year charter was established in 1924; it was named the Institut Sera-Vaccinogene. Modern medical legislation was enacted in 1930 and then implemented by the Ministry of the Interior.[21]

Occupation by the Italians from 1936 to 1941 was devastating for Ethiopians. The Italian government was only concerned with the health of their own soldiers, civilians, and close Ethiopian collaborators. A few immunization efforts for the general public were launched because Italian medical authorities were afraid that their people would be infected and return to Italy with contagious diseases. Italian medical staff took over hospitals built by the Ethiopian government and used them for their own subjects, reducing hospital beds for Ethiopian patients. The most consequential damage inflicted by the Italians was the killing of large numbers of educated Ethiopians.

After the Occupation, Haile Sellassie I regained control of the government despite efforts by the British to maintain their influence. He strengthened the administration of health matters by establishing the Ministry of Public Health in 1948, almost simultaneously with the founding of the World Health Organization and UNICEF.[22] Because of Haile Sellassie's leadership in the rise of these new international institutions, Ethiopia was able to mobilize significant human and financial resources from the international community.

Nevertheless, by the 1960s Ethiopia was still afflicted by many acute contagious diseases, especially diarrhea, dysentery, cholera, pneumonia, influenza, meningitis, typhus, polio, rabies, and relapsing fever.[23] Particularly at lower altitudes malaria, yellow fever, and sleeping sickness caused high morbidity and mortality.[24] Tuberculosis resulted in the death of tens of thousands.[25] Other long-term diseases, such as leprosy and onchocerciasis, disabled many.[26] Eye infections caused by trachoma and other infectious agents caused many to become blind.[27] Intestinal parasites infested a high percentage of the population.[28] Syphilis and gonorrhea were prevalent.[29] Fatalities and disabilities related to pregnancy and childbirth, such as hemorrhage, prolonged labor, and vesico-vaginal fistula, were common.[30] Acute injuries from accidents and conflicts killed many. Cardiovascular diseases, diabetes, and gout occasionally were seen, mainly in the affluent.[31] Mental illnesses of many types were common.[32]

In the 1950s, with few modern services available, all population groups in Ethiopian society (urban and rural, Christian, Muslim, and animist) relied on traditional healers. Various kinds of "specialists" focused on particular diseases and injuries. Some were primarily mechanical, such as the *wegasha* (bonesetter/surgeon) who used complicated splints for broken bones and dislocations in humans and animals. One set of technicians performed male circumcision, others did female genital cutting, uvula excision, and other procedures. Still other specialists administered secret potions for specific diseases and body organs. Some traveled about the countryside selling their secret mixtures of plants and other ingredients.[33] A large part of the population visited "holy water" (*tebel*) sites located near churches and other worship centers. Sick people would drink the water, wash themselves, or rest in the pool. These ablutions often were combined with prayer and seeking spiritual blessings from priests and monks, some of whom included exorcism of evil spirits. One famous monk exorcist in Woliso conducted daily healing services with more than seven million recorded visits during his forty year ministry.[34] Some church-related healers (*tenquaye*) made amulets to ward off sickness. Gondar was widely known as a city with many sites for traditional healing and was famous for training many kinds of healers. Some male healers who claimed to be possessed by powerful spirits (*balazar*) focused on the rural, female populations.[35] In almost every part of Ethiopia shamans known as *kalitcha* or *kalu* attracted large followings of people who wanted an expert to intercede in the spirit world on their behalf.[36]

Many diseases were endemic or epidemic in Kossoye in the 1960s. Malaria was not transmitted at Kossoye's 2900 meters above sea level, but villagers were exposed on visits to the lowlands. They knew the signs, symptoms, and seasons, and returned to the highlands before the end of the rainy season when most outbreaks occurred. Periodically fatal epidemics of meningitis, typhus, relapsing fever, and whooping cough swept the area around Kossoye. Water supply for household use was limited, unprotected, and highly contaminated, causing frequent diarrhea. The walls of the twenty-two houses in Cherema and Zinjero Wuha were constructed with locally grown indigenous trees and had grass for roofs and mud-plastered walls and floors. Little smoke escaped through the roofs, making air inside irritating and damaging to respiratory tracts. Most families brought domestic animals into the house at night for protection from wild animals and thieves. This led to a heavy domestic fly population around and in dwellings.

When Public Health College students and their supervisors began regular visits to Kossoye in 1963, villagers depended almost entirely on home remedies, traditional healers, and religious methods for treating illnesses and injuries of all kinds. Some Kossoyans traveled to Gondar or monasteries around Lake Tana with well known sites of "holy water." During one visit to Kossoye by students and teaching staff, a leading citizen with a chronic illness left the village to travel to a healing center at a distant monastery near Lake Tana, without requesting help for his illness from any of the modern health practitioners present in his home village. While many people in the countryside recognized the usefulness of modern medical practitioners, especially for immunizations and for managing acute infectious illnesses, large wounds, and prolonged labor, they believed traditional resources were more trustworthy for nearly everything else.

Student researchers learned the names and locations of many kinds of traditional healers in the Kossoye area.

One surgeon/bone setter (*wegesha*), Abebe Taye, lived near Cherema. Demissie Bogale in Medhane Alem knew the "uvula-shrinking practice." Wubineh Yetemegn, Taye's father, was skilled as a *wegesha* for animals, but worked mostly for relatives without payment. Taye's mother, Etenish Ingida, practiced as a traditional midwife. Taye's brother, Tagele Wubineh, claimed to know a prophylaxis for rabies derived from the root of an herb. Tembea Kebede charged 1.50 EB to make amulets to protect women and children from the "evil eye" (*buda*). *Debtera* Alemu was a diviner (*tenquai*) who used an old astrology book to diagnose and treat people. Aleka Tessema immigrated from Debre Tabor and worked as a diviner and *balazar* to treat "evil eye." Down in the lowlands Aleka Makonnen was another famous *balazar* who treated people afflicted by powerful spirits (*Zar*). Residents of Kossoye could choose from a wide range of traditional healers.[37]

The closest modern health facility was eight kilometers away in Ambaghiorgis, where a government clinic, staffed by a dresser with one or two years training, provided limited curative services. Taye didn't like the clinic because he thought the dresser didn't treat patients with adequate respect. He even threatened to sue the dresser responsible for these perceived insults in court, causing further alienation of Kossoyans from the closest modern health care facility.

This was the situation when students and staff from the Public Health College arrived in Kossoye. Students began collaborating with villagers to protect the main spring. They conducted regular home visits. They provided immunizations for diphtheria, whooping cough, and tetanus, as well as diagnoses and treatment of common ailments. Health education was promoted, local epidemics were managed, and annual mapping and census programs were accomplished. Sanitarian students built a demonstration pit latrine using cement, iron bars, and local materials. In retrospect the use of iron bars and cement (both non-local materials) was a major mistake, since the introduction of non-local materials effectively blocked the spread of latrine construction.[38]

During the time when these health services were being provided on a weekly basis, several health officer students working on their senior theses began local applied research projects. In addition to historical, economic, and nutritional inquiries, Alemayehu Abraha examined 110 Kossoye residents and found that 77% had eye infections, mostly trachoma; 84% had skin lesions, usually scabies in origin, but often complicated by secondary bacterial infections; 79% had at least one species of intestinal parasite; and many Kossoyans had more than one kind of worm.[39] Another student examined people for indications of louse infestation and found that 52% had lice in their clothes or hair.[40] Low standards of personal hygiene as well as inadequate environmental sanitation made Kossoyans highly vulnerable to infectious diseases. In the early 1960s modern health education and services had little or no impact on the lives of these peasants in the North Gondar region.

Nutrition

Ethiopia's nutritional status has been influenced by many factors, including marked fluctuations in rainfall, political governance, agricultural practices, epidemics of human and animal diseases, availability of emergency food, distribution of food within households, and child feeding practices. Most obvious has been the dramatically changing volume of rainfall and fluctuations of Nile River levels which affected northeastern Africa for at least four thousand years of recorded history. Dynasties in Egypt rose and fell according to the volumes of Nile flooding. Egyptians understood that the water of the Nile and the soil it carries are gifts from Ethiopia.[41] Over 80% of the Nile water originates in the Ethiopian highlands and is carried in the Blue Nile (*Abbai*).

The Tekeze and Baro-Sobaro rivers' contributions come from rains falling between May and October.[42] The major rainy season (*kremt*) in Ethiopia occurs when warm prevailing winds from the southeast pick up water from the Indian Ocean and meet cold air flowing from the European and Asian land masses.[43] The timing and intensity of the rainfall in Ethiopia varies greatly from year to year and closely correlates with recorded amounts that reach Egypt. Significant decreases in average rainfall may continue for two or three centuries with disastrous results for Egyptian populations and governments. At other times abundant rainfall has prevailed for several centuries. Shorter cycles of drought occur within long-term trends and influence agricultural production, food supplies, economies and political control.[44] An average of ten drought and famine periods per century has occurred in Ethiopia over the past seven hundred years of recorded history.[45]

Possibly the most destructive famine in modern Ethiopian history, "The Great Famine," took place from 1888 to 1892, when a dry and hot year preceded a rinderpest epidemic among cattle that spread countrywide and wiped out nearly all oxen. Ethiopian farmers were unable to cultivate their fields without their draft animals, and severe food shortages ensued. In a public effort to encourage peasants to work the soil by hand, Emperor Menelik II joined farmers using a hoe in the field. The Italian government took advantage of this period of social and economic chaos, when the population was weakened, to pursue its colonizing strategy on the northern highlands.[46] Taye's father, Wubineh Yetemegn, described "The Great Famine" in vivid terms in an interview in 1974. He was a small child during those harrowing years and told of the ecological chaos when "hyenas and lions attacked people."[47] Only after recovery from drought and rinderpest was well underway could Emperor Menelik mobilize military forces to fight and win the Battle of Adwa against a better-equipped Italian army.[48] Italy was humiliated among European colonial powers for losing a war to an African army.[49]

According to Collins, historian of the Nile River basin, the most disastrous droughts in five thousand years occurred in the twentieth century. He reports that people said "the river refused to flow in 1913, 1984, and 1987."[50] The Public Health College was called to respond to a serious regional drought in 1965 in Balessa and Ebinat, areas east of Gondar where famines and severe epidemics frequently occur. That year a student working with relief services surveyed 100 families and found that that 55% of those interviewed believed that the famine was "God's punishment for sins of the people." Another 18% thought that only "God knew the reason" why it occurred.[51] Kemant people from Balessa and Ebinat sometimes came to Kossoye seeking help. Residents of the highlands felt a strong obligation to give cereals to less fortunate relatives if the family ties were close.[52] Occasionally a lowlander tried to settle in the highlands if he could establish a hereditary right to cultivate and harvest his crops.

The highlands north of Gondar with altitudes over 2,500 meters above sea level were usually spared the worst effects of droughts since more rain falls at higher elevations. A food shortage was more likely to occur in the Kossoye highlands due to too much rain, rather than too little. In Kossoye the rainy season is almost always cold, with strong winds and rain. When the rain is heavy, a rot (*moog*) devastates crops and leaves residents with little to harvest.

Vitamin and mineral deficiencies affected large parts of the population in both the lowlands and highlands.[53] As most households consume few vegetables or fruit, vitamin A and C deficiencies are prevalent.[54] After birth, children are kept out of sunlight for months for fear of the "Evil Eye" and other spiritual entities (*mitch*), resulting in widespread vitamin D deficiencies, including severe rickets.

Other traditional practices in daily life also contribute to serious malnutrition in adults and children. The Ethiopian Orthodox Church requires fasting (abstaining from eating nearly all animal products) between 100 and 220 days per year.[55] Child feeding practices often hinder healthy growth and development of infants and children; butter and a heavy grain preparation are forcibly fed to newborn infants a few hours after delivery. Colostrum, the highly nutritious breast fluid that flows immediately after birth, is often discarded by mothers. Due to unsanitary food handling, infants and children suffer frequent gastrointestinal infections leading to poor appetite, low food intake, and loss of nutrients needed for healthy growth and maintenance. Diarrheal episodes occur so often in Kossoye that they are seen as practically normal.[56]

Scientific studies of nutritional conditions began as Haile Sellassie's modernization program gained momentum in the late 1940s and 1950s. A bilateral nutrition survey in eleven locations around the country was launched in 1957 by the Ethiopian government in collaboration with the United States International Committee on Nutrition for National Defense (ICNND). Some staff and students from the Public Health College were part of the program. The research revealed widespread protein/calorie deficiencies in many areas and estimates were made that adults ingested an average of 2,500 calories while doing hard work. They noted "excessive leanness" in adults and recommended that at least 400 additional calories be consumed each day. The final report stated that Vitamin A, C, and D deficiencies were widespread, as was iodine deficiency goiter. A national conference sponsored by the Emperor took place in 1959, and a wide variety of long-term measures were discussed and approved. Recommendations included establishing a national nutrition research institute.[57]

The Swedish government initiated a large long-term nutrition effort with the Ethiopian government in the late

1950s. The Child Nutrition Institute (later called the Ethio-pian Nutrition Institute) worked with the Pasteur Institute and the Ethio-Swedish Children's Clinic. Applied research projects carried out in several parts of the country focused on protein/calorie malnutrition, anemia, goiter, and other nutritional disorders. At the invitation of the Public Health College, Kossoye was one of the rural villages chosen for a week-long nutritional survey conducted by a research team from the Ethio-Swedish Nutrition Institute.[58]

Researchers made observations on the twelve Cherema and Zinjero Wuha families with children below the age of three years and studied the eating patterns of 78 people in those homes. They weighed food servings and took samples that were frozen at the Public Health College before being shipped by air to Uppsala University in Sweden. Detailed laboratory analysis indicated that toddlers six months to three years of age received only 38% of essential calories in the food they measured. Breast milk intake was not measured, and since nearly all children were breast-fed for at least two years, measurement of the total food intake of infants and young children was incomplete. Older children and adults received an average of 85% of required calories. Toddlers obtained 90% of their essential protein. Surprisingly the study showed that children and adults consumed 120% of the standard set for required proteins. Young children below three years ate or drank only 25% of required calcium, while older children and adults received 95% of calcium needed. Iron intake exceeded requirements for all ages.[59] Thiamine consumption reached adequate levels, and niacin was only mildly deficient. On the other hand, intakes of vitamins A and C were extremely low; toddlers consumed only 5% of normal daily requirements. Older children and adults ate 5% of required vitamin A and 30% of vitamin C in their regular diets, where they received some A and C from the hot chili spice (*berbere*). What little Vitamin A and C infants did eat came from legumes; many babies were also given butter.

Animal protein comprised only 8% of the total protein consumed. Flax seeds added some fat to the diet. The research team concluded: "The survey, which was conducted when the crops were harvested, and thus at a relatively favorable time of the year, nevertheless demonstrated gross dietary deficiencies. For older children and adults this was true, especially for Vitamin A and C. Compared to standard values used by the FAO and the WHO at the time, "for toddlers, calories, calcium and niacin were lacking to a serious degree."[60]

This kind of information was put to use by administrative, service, and teaching staff of the Public Health College. The College had to deal with epidemics, droughts, and famines in the Gondar region because its responsibilities included serving as the Provincial Health Department for an estimated two million people in the Begemder and Simen province. The Dean of the College was also the Provincial Medical Officer of Health.[61] Urgent calls for assistance with epidemics came frequently from remote districts, especially those at low altitudes such as Belessa, Ebinat, Qwara, Armacheho, and Janifankera. Teams of senior students and supervisors working in the "Far Field Program" were assigned to investigate and evaluate these emergency reports, recommend appropriate actions, and implement them when possible.

Many students chose topics for their senior research projects related to experiences they had in these outreach activities. Alemayehu Abraha, a senior in the Health Officer program, included nutritional measurements in his studies in Kossoye in 1965. Alemayehu divided the population into richer and poorer halves and compared weight gain per year. As expected, the 50% of males in the more affluent half of the population gained weight faster than those with fewer assets. Differences between rich and poor women were less than for males. Poor men gained weight at a slower rate than their wives.[62]

Another health officer student did an anthropometric study in 1967 that measured both height and weight of 101 out of 122 residents in Cherema and Zinjero Wuha.[63] When analyzed recently with a current statistical program, EPI Info, results showed that in 1967 17% of female children below 15 years and 20% of males under 15 were stunted, indicating long-term malnutrition. Among the females over 15 years of age, 15% were severely underweight. Among the males 15 years and older, 27% were severely underweight.[64]

Population and Family Planning

Although health services for rural communities like Kossoye were very limited in the 1950s and 1960s, even low and inadequate levels of modern health care contributed to a rapid increase in population. By the end of the 19th century there were no more than 5 million Ethiopians in the whole country.[65] In the early 1930s before the Italians invaded, estimates place the population at 6 to10 million.[66] By 1950 these figures had doubled to 15 million. In 1970 the total population reached 29.5 million.[67] Annual growth rates rose from an estimated 1.1% in 1930 to 1.8% in 1950, and 2.4% in 1970.[68]

In 1970 the infant mortality rate was estimated to be 151 per 1,000 live births in rural areas and 141 in urban locations. Total fertility rates were 5.15 live births per woman in rural Ethiopia and 3.14 in urban areas.[69] In his comparative studies of global demographic changes, Riley concluded that Ethiopia began its "health transition" in the 1940s and 1950s. He estimated that Ethiopians had an average life expectancy of about 30 years in 1950.[70] However, it seems likely that significant demographic transition was beginning in the rural areas around Gondar even before the Italian Occupation started in 1936.

Analysis of the health transition in Kossoye demonstrates the difficulty of balancing human interventions affecting nutrition and disease, on the one hand, with attitudes toward human fertility and family planning practices, on the other. In the 1950s in Ethiopia little attention was paid to these questions by responsible professional or political leaders. One study by Russell in 1956-1957 in the Gondar area was carried out to advise the government about organizing health services using mobile health teams; only incidentally were population statistics gathered. Russell and his colleagues did censuses in market towns, smaller roadside villages, and countryside villages in the Adi Arkai and Chilga areas, finding mean household size to be 3.3, and 48% of married couples having no children at all.[71]

The serious issue of rapid population growth was challenged in 1963 by Professor Cicely Williams in the keynote lecture to the first annual meeting of the Ethiopian Medical Association. She disputed arguments favoring family planning, saying that it was better to work for gradually improving health standards and reducing mortality rates. She stated, "More food, better and cheaper contraceptives, are to my thinking of minor importance. The major efforts should go into teaching parents respect for child life, confidence in children's survival, and pride in their future."[72] With this statement from a famous public health expert, it was understandable that medical professionals felt justified in blocking and resisting efforts to offer family planning as part of government health services.

Nevertheless, despite strong resistance by government and health professionals, in 1966 a few Ethiopians established the Family Guidance Association of Ethiopia (FGAE), with the support of international agencies such as the IPPFA. The FGAE began offering family planning services in Addis Ababa and training health professionals in necessary skills. Observing the large size of families in Kossoye and other rural areas, Carlson attempted to engage teaching staff and students in conversations about key issues and implications of rapid population growth for Ethiopia. He met strong resistance, especially from male teachers on the college faculty. He also raised the issue in conversations with both men and women in Kossoye. Most men and women were socially and economically conservative. At the family level, parents counted on their children to work at home to care for siblings, prepare food, carry water, and assist with herding and agriculture. With frequent deaths of infants and children, they could not risk having fewer children. Many did not want to change their way of life or status in the community, which they often believed was related to the number of children they could raise. As late as February 1974, shortly before the Revolution, Carlson had discussions with groups of Kossoye men and found no recognition that having many children might pose problems.[73]

Almost no rural women used family planning methods anywhere in Ethiopia in the 1960s. Few had even heard of methods of consciously limiting the number of pregnancies by safe and effective means. Rural and small town clinics, such as in Ambaghiorgis, had no trained staff or materials to offer such services. Nevertheless, concerns about economic development and population were important issues for Asfaw Desta and Dennis Carlson as they supervised students in Kossoye.[74] Using maps and census data, annually updated from 1963 to 1967, they compared the accuracy of data about births and deaths collected by local Orthodox priests and student census-takers and found that neither approach produced complete information, each missing events that the other method had recorded.

In 1967, while College students were carrying out the annual census of the Cherema and Zinjero Wuha community, a dramatic and unexpected conversation took place between Carlson and Shashitu Zewde, a forty-two-year old woman with seven children. Carlson recalls: "I was making supervisory visits to check on the accuracy of student interviews. When my colleague and I came to the home of Guangule Zeleke and Shashitu Zewde, we were invited to come in for a cup of coffee. Guangule was out farming, but as we waited for the coffee, heating on the open charcoal fire, Shashitu and I talked about her family. Gradually the subject shifted to questions about family size. Although it had not been my conscious intention to lead the conversation in this direction, I asked how many children she would like to have. She responded in the usual way, 'It is God's will. As many as He gives me.' Thinking that I might get a more informative response, I asked, 'If you could choose, how many more children would you want?' She nearly exploded with, 'I don't want more, I have enough already.' Delighted and surprised by the intensity of her answer, I asked her what would be her husband's reaction; she said he would support her decision. Then she declared, 'We are a poor family with many problems. We can't afford to support even the children we have.'"

Carlson continued: "I explained that there were several ways to prevent pregnancy, focusing especially on the insertion of an intrauterine device (IUD).[75] I suggested to her that we could bring equipment and supplies to Kossoye and provide services near her home. She was pleased and started to spread the news to her neighbors."[76]

That evening as the college staff rode back to Gondar, there was excited discussion about Shashitu's statement. Carlson recalled that "the supervisors felt we had discovered clues that might lead to better understanding of the population dynamics not only in Kossoye but the country as a whole; quite possibly there were large numbers of rural peasant women who would want to practice modern contraception if they had opportunity." The next day census forms were modified, and census-takers went back to interview fertile-aged women. Soon it became clear that women would be interested in contraception only if they had at least five living children, of which at least one was male. There were nine women in Cherema and Zinjero Wuha who met these criteria; three of the nine were not interested at all, and six showed strong interest. In addition to Shashitu, one of the most intensely interested women was Taye's wife, Semu, who had nine living children and said she was praying to God not to become pregnant again. Interviewers were able to find four of the six husbands; three said they would support the idea, including Taye. Berihun did not want his wife to limit pregnancy.

The possibility of contraception that could be reversed later if desired was discussed widely in the community as preparations were made for a one-day family planning session in the schoolhouse (classes met out-of-doors that day). Kes Eshete Bogale, the priest and the local judge (*atbia dagna*) for the Kossoye area, declared that contraception was "a miracle."[77] His wife had delivered eight live births already and was pregnant with the ninth at the time. But he assured the college staff that his wife would come for an IUD insertion as soon she had delivered her ninth child.

Two women whose husbands were not available for interviewing claimed that it did not matter what their husbands thought; even if their husbands had children by other women, they wouldn't mind. When asked why they wanted to avoid pregnancy, one said she was afraid of dying in childbirth, and the other replied that her family was so poor she couldn't provide decent clothes for her children, even for holidays.[78]

On the appointed day in July, sheets were hung on wires in the classroom, and a desk served as the treatment table. Only the minimum of equipment was available, since the planners thought that possibly a precedent was being set for similar efforts in other rural settings: intra-uterine-contraceptive devices (IUDs), speculum, tenaculum, forceps, plastic insertion tube, flashlight, disinfectant, and rubber gloves.[79] Four of the six women who previously said they wanted to begin family planning arrived and the contraceptive devices were inserted with minimal difficulty.[80]

Several community nurses were trained in IUD insertion in the college outpatient clinic and made follow-up visits to

Kossoye to see if other women wanted to begin. Kes Eshete's wife was visited at home after her delivery but refused an IUD because she believed it would be interfering with God's will. For unknown reasons Semu, Taye's wife, received an IUD but later had it removed. By the time Semu reached menopause she had delivered a total of eleven live infants, two more after 1967.

Conclusion

In the 1960s, as the dynamics of economic growth and health development became more clearly understood and demographic studies were conducted worldwide, international concern about population growth increased. In Ethiopia, however, there was strong resistance to family planning. Indeed in national policy circles the prevailing opinion favored robust population growth, particularly because of a perceived need for military manpower. This was coupled with a belief that nearly unlimited land was available for any "surplus" population. Although the Public Health College and Training Centre's purposes included demonstrating model health services and preparing personnel for staffing health centers, there was almost no support among the academic staff for teaching family planning. On several occasions Carlson tried to introduce the issue into curriculum discussions, but he was rebuffed. Systematic theoretical teaching did not take place in the classroom about the relationship of population growth to health, nutrition, and economic development, nor did practical training occur except as related to Kossoye.

Access to health services was improving slowly but was unreliable and usually inaccessible. Thus traditional attitudes remained. Even in Kossoye, the most innovative thinker, Taye Wubineh, did not see a need to limit family size. Although he had two daughters with his first wife, then another seven children with his second wife, his wife used an IUD for only a short time. In 1967 at the age of 43 she gave birth to twin boys, making Taye father for eleven children. His substantial wealth in land and cattle may have given him confidence that all his progeny would be set up well in life. The arithmetic of peasant farming in northern Ethiopia, in which an average family needed about four hectares of land and two oxen, indicated that even Taye's ample resources would not be adequate for the next generation.

Notes

1. Simon Kuznets, "Recent Population Trends in Less Developed Countries and Implications for Internal Income Inequality," in *Population and Economic Change in Developing Countries,* Richard A. Easterlin, ed. (Chicago and London: University of Chicago Press, 1980): 470-474.

2. Thomas McKeown, "Food, Infection, and Population," in *Hunger and History: The Impact of Changing Food Production and Consumption Patterns on Society*, Robert I. Rotberg and Theodore K. Rabb, eds. (Cambridge: Cambridge University Press, 1983), 29-41.

3. Nevin S. Scrimshaw, "Functional Consequences of Malnutrition for Human Populations: A Comment," in *Hunger and History,* 211-214; Carl E. Taylor, "Synergy among Mass Infections, Famines, and Poverty," in *Hunger and History,* 285-305.

4. Richard Pankhurst, *An Introduction to the Medical History of Ethiopia* (Trenton: The Red Sea Press, 1990), chapters 3, 4, 5, 14.

5. Richard Pankhurst, "The Great Ethiopian Famine of 1888-1892: A New Assessment," *Journal of the History of Medicine and Allied Sciences,* Vol. 21 (1966), 95-124, 271-294.

6. Pankhurst, *An Introduction to the Medical History,* 149.

7. Pankhurst, *An Introduction to the Medical History,* 139.

8. Pankhurst, *An Introduction to the Medical History,* 139.

9. Pankhurst, *An Introduction to the Medical History,* 140.

10. Pankhurst, *An Introduction to the Medical History*, 141-154.

11. Roland Oliver and J. D. Fage, *A Short History of Africa* (New York: New York University Press, 1962, 1964), 181-195.

12. Pankhurst, *An Introduction to the Medical History*, 158-162.

13. Pankhurst, *An Introduction to the Medical History*, 167,170.

14. Pankhurst, *An Introduction to the Medical History*, 170-173.

15. Pankhurst, *An Introduction to the Medical History*, 171-172.

16. Pankhurst, *An Introduction to the Medical History*, 166.

17. Variolation is the practice of inoculating non-immune people with pus from a person sick with smallpox. Though it was practiced in Asia, India, and parts of Africa for many centuries, the practice gained popularity in the 18th century in Europe. See Fielding Garrison, *An Introduction to the History of Medicine* (Philadelphia: W.B.Saunders, 1966, 4th Edition), 405.

18. Pankhurst, *An Introduction to the Medical History*, chap. 17.

19. Pankhurst, *An Introduction to the Medical History*, 212.

20. Pankhurst, *An Introduction to the Medical History* , 205.

21. Pankhurst, *An Introduction to the Medical History*, chap. 18.

22. Asrat Waldeyes, in Pankhurst, *An Introduction to the Medical History*.

23. Charles P. Larson and Tigest Ketsela, "Acute Childhood Diarrhea," in *The Ecology of Health and Disease in Ethiopia*, Helmut Kloos and Zein Ahmed Zein, eds. (Boulder: Westview Press, 1993), 203-212.

24. Assefa Nega Tulu, "Malaria," 341-352; Merid Mekonnen and Helmut Kloos,"Yellow Fever," 389-398; Ephraim Mamo, "Trypanosomiasis," 353-366, in *The Ecology of Health and Disease in Ethiopia*.

25. Richard M. Hodes and Mogues Azbite, "Tuberculosis," in *The Ecology of Health and Disease in Ethiopia*, 265-284.

26. Debre Berhe, Rawleigh C. Howe, Tadele Tedla, and Dominique Frommel, "Leprosy," 251-264; Ahmed Zein, "Onchocerciasis," 367-374, in *The Ecology of Health and Disease in Ethiopia*.

27. Wondu Alemayehu and Assefa Cherinet, "Eye Diseases and Blindness," in *The Ecology of Health and Disease in Ethiopia*, 237-250.

28. Helmut Kloos and Tesfa-Michael Tesfa-Yohannes, "Intestinal Parasitism," in *The Ecology of Health and Disease in Ethiopia*, 223-235.

29. Workneh Feleke and Helmut Kloos, "Sexually Transmitted Diseases," in *The Ecology of Health and Disease in Ethiopia*, 295-306.

30. M.E.Duncan, Letebirhan Mehari, Gerard Tibaux, and Andre Pelzer, "Social Aspects of Obstetrics and Gynecology," in *The Ecology of Health and Disease in Ethiopia*, 307-318.

31. Frances T. Lester, "Chronic Noninfectious Diseases of Adults," 427-438; Frances T. Lester, "Diabetes Mellitus," 439-448, in *The Ecology of Health and Disease in Ethiopia*.

32. Mesfin Araya and Frances Aboud, "Mental Illness," in *The Ecology of Health and Disease in Ethiopia*, 493-506.

33. Richard Pankhurst, *An Introduction to the History of Medicine*, 113-120.

34. Dennis Carlson visited Aba Wolde Tensaye in Woliso in 1961 and again in 1990. Probably the most famous monk/exorcist in modern Ethiopia, Aba Wolde Tensaye (Father Son of the Resurrection) kept complete records of all the people who came to him through the more than 30 years he conducted his preaching and healing. By the late 1990s he claimed to have had more than 7 million visits by Ethiopians from all over the country.

35. Simon D. Messing, *The Target of Health in Ethiopia* (New York: MSS Information Corporation, 1972), 228-241.

36. Karl Eric Knutsson, *Authority and Change: A Study of the Kallu Institution Among the Macha Galla of Ethiopia* (Goteborg: Etnografiska Museet, 1967), 65-93; Karl Eric Knutsson, "Possession and Extra-institutional Behavior," *Ethnos*, 40: I-IV (1975), 244-272.

37. Tadelle Mengesha, "Report on Social and Psychological Patterns of People at Cherema and Zenjero Wuha" (unpublished paper, Haile Sellassie I Public Health College and Training Centre, August 1964), 7-9.

38. The use of cement and iron bars along with locally available wood and stones followed the accepted "orthodoxy" of latrine construction in that period. However dependence on materials from outside the immediate community defeated any expectation that residents would imitate this construction since even the relatively low costs of cement and iron bars were beyond the capability and imagination of the residents.

39. Alemayehu Abraha, "Health in the Low and High Socio-Economic Groups in Kossoye with a Brief Review on the History, Geography, and Economy," (unpublished paper, Haile Sellassie I Public Health College and Training Centre, 1965), 24-26.

40. Anonymous, unpublished student research paper, 5.

41. Haggai Erlich, *The Cross and the River: Ethiopia, Egypt and the Nile* (Boulder: Lynne Rienner, 2002), 3.

42. Robert O. Collins, *The Nile* (New Haven: Yale University Press, 2002), 13; Erlich, *The Cross and the River*, 1. Erlich states that 86% of the Nile flow comes from Ethiopia.

43. Collins, *The Nile*, 13.

44. Collins, *The Nile*, 19.

45. Richard Pankhurst, "The Great Ethiopian Famine of 1888-1892: A New Assessment," *Journal of the History of Medicine and Allied Sciences*, 21(1966), 95-124, 271-94.

46. Pankhurst, "The Great Ethiopian Famine."

47. Dennis G. Carlson, "Famine in History: With A Comparison of Two Modern Ethiopian Disasters," in *Famine*, Kevin M. Cahill ed. (Orbis Maryknoll, 1982), 9-11. Born in 1887, Wubineh was five years old when the Great Famine had run its course. Carlson interviewed him in 1974 and was struck by the passion with which the elderly gentleman retold the story as if the event was a recent happening.

48. Carlson, "Famine in History," 5-16.

49. Richard Greenfield, *Ethiopia: A New Political History* (New York: Frederick Praeger, 1965), 123.

50. Collins, *The Nile*, 23.

51. Tsegaye Tekle, "An Economic and Demographic Survey of Some Famine Refugees in Begemidir-Simien Province," (unpublished paper, Haile Sellassie I Public Health College and Training Centre, 1966).

52. Interview 73, February 15, 2006.

53. The precise nature of *moog* has been difficult to determine. Some claim it is due to a "cut worm." Others simply refer to it as "rot."

54. In conversation with Dennis Carlson (March 2005), Professor Yigzaw Kebede related that Kemant farmers close to Gondar city grew vegetables extensively in recent decades and that he had earned his way through secondary school in Gondar by selling fresh vegetables at Saturday markets.

55. Aberra Bekele, Zewdie Wolde-Gebriel, and Helmut Kloos, "Food, Diet, and Nutrition," in *The Ecology of Health and Disease in Ethiopia*, 90.

56. Repeated morbidity studies have shown that children still suffer an average of five episodes of diarrhea per year.

57. "Ethiopia Nutrition Survey: A Report by the Interdepartmental Committee on Nutrition for National Defense," Washington D.C., 1959.

58. Ruth Selinus, Guenet Awalom, Abeba Gobezie, "Dietary Studies in Ethiopia. II Dietary Pattern in Two Rural Communities in N. Ethiopia, A Study with Special Attention to the Situation in Young Children," *Acta Societatis Medicorum Upsaliensis*, LXXX, (1971), 1-2.

59. Selinus et al., "Dietary Studies." Teff (Eragrostis tef) is the most favored cereal grain in highland Ethiopia and is used mainly for making *injera*. It is of excellent nutritional value with an unusually high content of iron. For many years debate continued whether the high iron content was intrinsic in the grain or was a contaminant due to harvesting on hardened bare ground and came from the soil. The debate seems settled that teff does contain significantly high

iron in and of itself. The Ethio-Swedish nutritional research team noted that Kossoyans primarily grew various kinds of barley and wheat, with lesser amounts of sorghum and teff. Chick peas, field peas and lentils were harvested. Oil seeds such as niger (*Guizotia abbysinica*) and flax seed (*Linum usi tatissimum*) are also grown.

60. Selinus et al, "Dietary Studies," 1-2.

61. Dennis Carlson was appointed Dean and Director in 1964.

62. Alemayehu Abraha, "Health in the Low and High Socioeconomic Groups," 15-24.

63. Anonymous, "Health Indicators in Kossoye," (unpublished research paper, Haile Sellassie I Public Health College and Training Centre, 1967).

64. These 1967 height and weight data recorded by the anonymous health officer student was analyzed in 2005 using the EPI/INFO 6 program.

65. Paul B. Henze, *Layers of Time: A History of Ethiopia* (London: Hurst, 2000), 184.

66. Henze, *Layers of Time*, 210.

67. Henze, *Layers of Time*, 270,

68. Assefa Hailemariam and Helmut Kloos, "Population," in *The Ecology of Health and Disease in Ethiopia*, 47-66.

69. Assefa Hailemariam and Helmut Kloos, "Population," in *The Ecology of Health and Disease in Ethiopia*, 47-66.

70. James C. Riley, "The Timing and Pace of Health Transitions Around the World," *Population and Development Review*, 31(4) (December 2005), 761.

71. H.B.L.Russell, "Population Study of the Begemider Province of Ethiopia," *Ethiopian Medical Journal*, 5:2 (January 1967), 85-111.

72. Cicely Williams, "Population Explosion," *Ethiopian Medical Journal*, 1:5, 246-253.

73. Dennis Carlson, unpublished Field Notes, February 1974.

74. Asfaw Desta and Dennis Carlson, Unpublished paper (Gondar, Ethiopia: 1967).

75. Mechanical contraceptive devices were not widely available in Ethiopia in 1967. Lippes loops were the most common intrauterine contraceptive devices available at the time.

76. Dennis Carlson conversation with Andrew Carlson, 1994.

77. Conversation between *Kes* Eshete Bogale and Dennis Carlson, July 1967.

78. Dennis G. Carlson, "An Exploration of Attitudes Toward Fertility Control in a Traditional Rural Community," Annual Public Health Conference, Haile Sellassie I Public Health College, June 1967.

79. Lippes Loops were the type of IUDs used in Cherema in 1967 and only available on a very limited basis.

80. To the best of our knowledge this was the first time family planning services were provided in Ethiopia in a rural community where there was no health facility.

CHAPTER FIVE

REVOLUTION

❖ ❖ ❖

In 1974 Haile Sellassie had been Emperor for forty-four years, one of the longest reigns in Ethiopia's very long history. He had built up a national educational system that had attracted a large group of international professionals and created a middle class. He had helped extend modernization from urban areas into peasant society by building rural elementary schools and health centers. The population had grown from about 10 million in 1930 to nearly 30 million in 1970. In short, Haile Sellassie's leadership provided Ethiopia with remarkable stability and international prestige through some of the most difficult decades of the twentieth century. Then on September 12, 1974, Haile Sellassie was formally deposed, and Ethiopia was on its way into a revolution that would profoundly change life in Kossoye and other rural communities.[1]

In retrospect, it is difficult to overstate the challenges Haile Sellassie faced as a modernizing monarch. The state modernization plan that he inherited from Tewodoros, Yohannes IV, and Menelik II focused on strengthening the center by diminishing the power of regional kings and nobles, and building a strong military. Over time fewer rivals emerged from the nobility to assume the mantle of Emperor. After Crown Prince Asfa Wossen suffered a debilitating stroke in January 1973, there was no clear successor for the octogenarian Emperor. One hundred twenty years of centralization and consolidation had vastly diminished the power and ambition of the nobility, resulting in a contraction of Ethiopia's options for aristocratic leadership.

Of course, ideas of democracy and popular sovereignty had also taken root, especially among students and the middle class. This was a global trend, not just an Ethiopian one. In the 1970s middle-class dissatisfaction with the Emperor and the existing feudal society intensified dramatically. One major complaint was the Emperor's neglect of the famine in 1973, when tens of thousands of rural people starved to death. Another aggravation was the rising price of oil, as the world entered a supply crisis following the Arab-Israeli War. Town and city dwellers depended on modern transportation and commerce. In early 1974 strikes and protests by professional military officers, teachers, students, taxi drivers, and assorted clerks and administrators created a sense of crisis. These groups voiced different grievances, most of them economic, but ultimately the blame focused on Ethiopia's monarch and the feudal society. From the middle-class perspective it seemed that Ethiopia's government was only meeting the needs of its nobility, not the broader society.

Even in this context, the historian Bahru Zewde notes that the revolution, which started in February of 1974, "caught almost everybody by surprise."[2] There were many models of revolutions: American, French, Russian, and Chinese. Educated Ethiopians were well aware that societies have often entered modernity through revolutions that radically reshaped the social and political order.[3] In some sense an American model had been tried in Ethiopia, making more attractive the political theories of Marx and Lenin that addressed the dual problems of aristocratic privilege and peasant exploitation.

The Emperor's government responded to the criticism and unrest with a series of directives. A relief commission addressed the food shortages in the famine-stricken northern highlands and southern lowlands. Military pay was increased. Cabinet members and the prime minister were replaced. The reform government proposed changes to the 1955 constitution that would have provided an English-style constitutional monarchy with greater civil liberties. A special commission was appointed to investigate official corruption. Plans were announced for land reform, including provisions that henceforward only peasants would receive land grants, and landholdings would be limited to 1000 hectares. Press censorship was lifted.

While these incremental steps were in many ways positive, they were not enough to slow the mobilization of the military against the government. Bahru Zewde observes that military interventions were not new in Ethiopian history.[4] Like his predecessors, Haile Sellassie had depended on the military to defend the center against aristocratic competitors and to control the border lands. The Eritrean rebellion, begun after the Emperor voided its autonomous status in 1961, had necessitated a stronger military. The Ogaden region bordering Somalia also required a military presence. What distinguished Haile Sellassie from Menelik and Tewodoros was that he had to contend with a larger, more organized, and better educated military as well as a cadre of junior and non-commissioned officers seething with class resentment of aristocratic senior officers.

In late June 1974, a group of young officers called for a convention of military representatives from service regiments. They called themselves "The Coordinating Committee of the Armed Forces." This group came to be known as "the committee" (*Derg*). Among the many who spoke at the convention was Major Mengistu Haile Mariam from the Harar Third Division. The speeches had little class rhetoric. The slogan that came out of that meeting was "Ethiopia above all" (*Etiopia Tikdem*) —a phrase calling for national unity. The *Derg* also called for members of the old regime to resign. The Emperor found himself between his military and his old and new governments, and it seems that he did not have the foresight or support to restrain the *Derg*. While his ministers went into hiding or exile and his latest cabinet resigned, officers from the Fourth Division occupied the palace. For several months they lived in the palace with the Emperor, making proclamations of their loyalty to him while also criticizing his corruption and incompetence. On September 12, 1974, his legitimacy sufficiently weakened, Haile Sellassie was deposed.

The new Provisional Military Administrative Council (PMAC) announced the end of feudalism by abolishing parliament and suspending the constitution. From 1974 to 1976, neither the junior officers nor the rest of the middle class had a clear vision of where the revolution would take Ethiopia. Through a series of murderous purges within the *Derg*, Colonel Mengistu Haile Mariam asserted his authority and eliminated Ethiopia's other civilian, left-leaning parties. The country and the world were shocked in November 1974 to learn of the summary execution of 59 former senior officials and members of the royal family. The death of the Emperor, by strangulation, came in September of 1975.[5]

One distinctive feature of Mengistu's rise to power was his incorporation of Marxist-Leninist ideology into the *Derg's* political agenda. This was not part of the *Derg's* initial program under the "Ethiopia First" (*Etiopia tikdem)* motto used to galvanize the masses and provide patriotic cover in 1974 and 1975. Leftist parties and ideology became so dominant that in order to defend their position as guardians of the revolution, Mengistu and the military had to ideologize their agenda. After December 1974 the PMAC issued a series of declarations on socialism that confirmed Ethiopia's shift to Russian and Chinese revolutionary models, called for a one-party state, and nationalized land and private property.

There are no contemporaneous written reports from Kossoye for the years between 1974 and 1992. As the revolution turned violent, American and European faculty members left the Gondar Public Health College, replaced in some instances by Russians, Cubans, East Germans, North Koreans, and Chinese. Thus this part of the story of the revolution in Kossoye is constructed entirely from retrospective accounts given in interviews since 1994.

Christopher Clapham describes the history of peasants during this period as one of "*encadrement*, or incorporation into structures of control, which was pursued with remarkable speed and ruthlessness."[6] The vastly expanded state authority was defended as necessary for modernization and development of Ethiopia's backward peasants. By 1991 most Kossoyans had come to feel that their lives were poorer and meaner than before the Revolution.

Reform from Above

The *Derg* approach to development in rural Ethiopia was qualitatively different from that taken in the 1960s by the Haile Sellassie I College of Public Health and Training Centre. Both approaches involved top-down mandates, although Haile Sellassie took the posture of the encouraging father figure, while Mengistu dictated. Both approaches also involved outside expertise, first from the West, then from the Soviet Union, Cuba, and China. But treatment of rural people was singularly different. Before the *Derg* took power, students and faculty members from the college were using the bottom-up principle that the community should establish priorities, such as protecting springs in order "to make better *tella*." Hence the focus was to identify local innovators and leaders such as Taye and Shashitu, who led in starting the school, growing eucalyptus trees, and practicing family planning. The *Derg* approach, in contrast, was to deliver a plan without any discussion or input. The Kossoyans thus became objects of reform—pawns to be moved about in a reconfigured social landscape—rather than collaborators in development. Modernization and development were to come by force, rather than collaboration.

The first of the *Derg* reformers came to Kossoye in early 1975 as part of the "Development Through Cooperation Campaign." Most were students from urban areas charged with conducting a literacy campaign and instructing peasants in Marxist ideology, especially the benefits of nationalizing land and other property. A hidden aim of the campaign (*zemetcha*) was to remove high school and college students from urban areas where they could be most disruptive. Since most adults in Kossoye were illiterate, the *zemetcha* addressed a real need. In later years, when asked if they had education, many adult Kosssoyans would say that they had not been to school but had attended the *zemetcha*. For example, one 31-year-old farmer said: "I know how to read and write through the literacy campaign, as did my brother."[7] Virtually none commented on ideological training, although they reported that participation was forced.[8]

The second wave of reformers in Kossoye came later in 1975 with a more ambitious agenda: land reform. Since 1965, high school and college students had been marching under the slogan, "Land to the Tiller." The *Derg's* "Proclamation to Provide for the Public Ownership of Rural Lands" did not disappoint the most radical reformers. Whereas earlier in 1974 Haile Sellassie's reform cabinet had proposed a limit of 1000 hectares for individual landholdings, in March 1975 the *Derg* "abolished all forms of private land ownership and prohibited the sale, lease or mortgage of rural land."[9] All tenancy was abolished. Peasants' landholdings could not exceed 10 hectares.

Obviously, redistribution could not be enforced from afar, particularly given the traditional power structures in rural Ethiopia in which land and government office went hand in hand. Thus in 1975 and 1976, as the *Derg* consolidated power, the Provisional Government of Ethiopia began to find new leaders to manage the localities, which were divided into urban *kebeles* and rural peasant associations. These new leaders became the local elite, charged with bringing a socialist revolution to rural Ethiopia. Among the outsiders, many were Ministry of Agriculture employees. Some local people also saw an opportunity to get ahead by taking newly created positions in the Peasant Association. The militia, armed with Kalashnikov machine guns, protected the community from bandits and backed up the authority of the governing committee members and chairman.

The effects of land reform in the Kossoye parish were dramatic. Land ownership was the foundation of the economy and society. While there were no local aristocrats with large land holdings, people did distinguish between the rich and poor. Few individuals owned more than 10 hectares, 4 oxen, and even 50 cows and sheep. The average holding in the 1960s was approximately 3 or 4 hectares, with 1 or 2 oxen and 15 cows and sheep. There were also families with no land or livestock who labored for wealthier farmers or worked as artisans. The first settlers in Cherema and Zinjero Wuha were relatively well off, and so they lost the most land and livestock. Usually the confiscated pieces of land were those farthest removed from their homes. Farmers with middling land holdings were less affected because they had less to lose. The poorest local residents, with nothing to lose, found their positions improved.

In Kossoye there was not a dramatic changeover in the ownership of cultivated fields, since most farmers maintained the parcels of land closest to their primary residences. In 1977 Guangule Zelleke, who had inherited (*rist)* lands in both Cherema and Ambaras, chose to move to his better land in Ambaras.[10] Another farmer, 70 years old in 1994, reported that he had parcels in many different places, but "the *Derg* took land for villagization and redistributed other pieces."[11]

Kes Sisay, the priest at the local Bata Mariam Church and Taye's oldest son, recounted how land reform changed his family fortunes. His grandfather, Wubineh, had 30 *tind* of land (8 or 9 hectares), eight oxen, and some 30 cows. His own father also had about 10 hectares, 50 sheep, and more than 50 cows. Much of this land was in the Ambaras area, where Sisay's next younger brother had moved. The family lost much of its land there, but the brother retained 10-12 *tind* of very fertile land. Sisay reported: "Now I have six cows, two to three oxen, one calf, five sheep (had 20 but 15 died). I have eight *tind*—but it is not fertile land. I have a peasant who does the farming. I spend most of my time at the church."[12]

Taye was able to keep about half of his land in the family by setting up his children on various parcels. If one goes by the rule of thumb that 1 hectare is four *tind*, Sisay now had 2 hectares and his brother 3 hectares, while their grandfather had 8 or 9 hectares and their father more than 10 hectares. Other sons, and perhaps daughters, who were already married by 1975 also received small parcels.

The story of a young man who had lived in a neighboring parish is especially poignant. Before the *Derg* his father had been a wealthy farmer with more than 100 *tind* (25 hectares) and 70 cows, oxen, and sheep. But when his father accidentally shot a nephew, around the time of the Revolution, his uncle forced his brother to give over all his land "as a price for the blood of his son" and never return to the area, "even for the funeral of his children." The uncle subsequently lost the land in the time of the redistribution, but the damage to the family had been done. The father left his family to be a security guard for the Ministry of Agriculture; his wife became a nun; three of his four sons were forced into military service, one never to return. The youngest son, 29 years old at the time of the interview, found himself supporting an extended family of 11 people (two brothers, the family of the deceased brother, a wife, and one child) on five *tind* of land (a little more than one hectare). "I couldn't get good land since I didn't have the money [for a bribe]. Even the members of the

Peasant Association gave me a nickname of the 'Young Man Who Comes with a White Paper.' Because I wrote them that I didn't have money. After that I started to work, but my crop production would not feed my family for a year. It was problematic for me."[13]

Nationalization also extended to other capital goods, notably eucalyptus trees. Taye was able to keep the plot of land where he had begun his original eucalyptus nursery on the edge of Cherema but the trees were cut and sold, and the government took the money. In 1977 local *Derg* officials established a tree nursery near the Medhane Alem Church, in essence taking the good idea from Taye. Kes Eshete Bogale, who had served as *atbia dagna* in the feudal era, was employed as the supervisor, becoming an employee of the Ministry of Agriculture. Over the next several years he planted indigenous tree species as well as eucalyptus. For several years these seedlings were given free to schools and churches in Wagera, Gondar, and Chilga. Then in 1988 a private market developed, with 30-50 seedlings selling for one EB. Meanwhile, more families used their plots to plant eucalyptus trees for sale as a cash crop.[14]

Land reform negatively affected those farmers who had been most closely associated with the feudal government. For a time, Taye retained the elevated status of *chika shum* and *shambel* by being elected as Chairman of the new Farmer's Association. In this capacity he purchased a community grinding mill. But by the late 1970s, after he lost much of his land and trees, Taye took a lower profile in the community, perhaps as a result of his objections to Marxist-style reforms. In his brother-in-law's words: "We have regressed. The *Derg* oppressed us very much. It did not allow us to make any-thing. How can you get development when they take your property?"[15]

Nationalization and redistribution also impacted institu-tions within the community. The school was allocated 60 *tind* (15 hectares) by the Farmer's Association, much more than the ten *tind* standard set by the *Derg*. Another 12 *tind* was added in 1990, demonstrating strong local commitment to education.[16] Parents plowed the land and planted crops and eucalyptus trees, providing the school with some income.

The churches did not do so well. Bata Mariam and Tsion Mariam were left with only ten *tind* of land.[17] Medhane Alem, which was farther from the road, retained 80 *tind* (20 hectares), much of it planted in eucalyptus trees.[18] During the *Derg* regime the people around Medhane Alem Church, virtually all of Kemant ancestry, were successful in arguing that the church lands were "the people's lands." The cash received from eucalyptus sales provided the whole parish with a significant source of income.

The nationalization of land changed life in Kossoye. Of course it remained an agricultural society, dependent upon traditional technologies, but the redistribution of land made subsistence more difficult for wealthier farmers like Taye. The new 10-hectare ceiling on landholdings was not onerous, since in Kossoye anyone with that much land was considered wealthy. The largest landholding was 25 hectares, owned by someone on the outskirts of the parish community. In the context of the highly populated northern highlands where arable land was in short supply, the new standard after redistribution was 1-3 hectares (4-12 *tind*). Even in the best of circumstances this was barely enough land to make a subsistence living.

There were at least two positive aspects of land reform. One was the termination of land litigation, a practice that consumed a great deal of time and money on the part of ordinary people, who often inherited legal suits with lands. Even farmers who lost land and deeply resented the *Derg* regime considered this an achievement.[19]

A second accomplishment was that Kossoye became a more equal society. While the goal of material equality was not achieved by land reform, economic stratification was diminished. The poorest of the poor had access to land. The

Falashas, who had not owned land in the Kossoye area, were given plots. The Kemant, as a whole, also benefited from land redistribution, because they had been at a disadvantage to the Amhara, not simply in the inheritance of lands, but also in legal disputes about land rights. A consequence was that hostilities between the Amhara and Kemant diminished.[20]

Removing land as private property had a significant impact on dowries and inheritance practices. The retention of usufructuary rights did not guarantee that parents could pass on land to children, although farmers continued to think of land as their private (and inheritable) property.[21] Wealthier families lost multiple plots, and families with only one plot had the problem of dividing this between several children. The greatest disadvantage, however, fell on girls, who previously could count on land as part of their inheritance. The leveling in rural wealth that came with the revolution meant that Kossoye families could not keep several plots of land in different places over several generations. Now land had to be occupied and local government support for one's claims maintained.

For Taye's children the transition was relatively easy, since he distributed parcels to his many sons before the Revolution. For his grandchildren, however, the consequences were much harder. Either they would divide family holdings of 1-3 hectares upon the deaths of their parents, or they would plead with the local government for an allotment. In thinking about his children's future professions in 1994, Taye's oldest son, Kes Sisay, said he did not want them to be farmers or priests, but rather believed they should pursue education, even if it meant leaving the area.[22]

Mengistu's Tyranny

The years between 1975 and 1977 were relatively open compared to what would follow after 1978, when Mengistu asserted tighter control of the *Derg* and shut down public discussion about Ethiopia's future. Parties were banned. The Red Terror eliminated or imprisoned party leaders and activists. Tens of thousands of middle class individuals left the country, walking or driving to Somalia, Sudan, Djibouti, or Kenya. Hundreds of Ethiopians who were studying in the United States decided it was not safe to return home. Communication and technical assistance programs from Europe and North America were severely reduced.

In Gondar and on university and college campuses around the country public life became dangerous. The Gondar-based *Derg* political leader, Major Melaku Teferra, ordered scores of people imprisoned and killed. Some bodies were reported to have been buried at the base of the Kemant sacred mountain (Jigeru) near Kossoye and eucalyptus trees planted over them. Many students and faculty members made plans to leave the country, taking with them valuable education and experience. As the war with Eritrea intensified, the focus at the college hospital became treating wounded soldiers.

The Public Health College's emphasis on health for under-served, mainly rural populations should have found a prominent place in Ethiopia's new Marxist political universe, but paradoxically the national paradigm shifted to higher priority being given to modern clinical medicine. Ironically, one of the early health officer students in Kossoye, Tadelle Mengesha, was a top administrator at the Ministry of Health when the decision was made to transform the public health college into a medical school. Advisors from the Soviet Union and Cuba recommended that a higher quality of comprehensive health care would be given if physicians were in charge at every level. Some health officer alumni of the College joined in the reform movement. Ultimately this turning away from public health to clinical medicine led to a significant loss of benefits for the country's rural population, which was beginning to be served by a comprehensive approach to improving health based on rural health centers. Physicians graduating from the Gondar, Addis Ababa, and later Jimma medical schools refused to make long-term commitments to serve in rural hospitals or health centers.[23] The last year that health officers graduated in Gondar was 1978, the year that the College stopped having an active presence in Kossoye.

In 1984 the Worker's Party of Ethiopia (WPE) became "the last ruling communist party to be created anywhere in the world, before the debacle of 1989...."[24] Three years later the government formally changed its name to The People's Democratic Republic of Ethiopia, completing the shift to a one-party totalitarian state. Mengistu was not only head of the Worker's Party of Ethiopia, but also the president of the country.

The celebration of the Revolution's 10th anniversary in 1984 was accompanied by a series of tragic events. As the guerilla campaigns in Tigray and Eritrea continued, the country was afflicted by a severe drought which led to the disastrous famine of 1984-85, affecting eight million people, one million of whom died. Meanwhile, Mengistu spent lavishly on the anniversary celebration, with many international guests and observers in Addis Ababa. A few weeks later, the world began to learn of the human devastation. International pressure forced the government to accept food and other assistance from Europe and North America, thus opening practically the whole society to western influences.

The northern highlands around Kossoye, however, remained closed to international visitors because of fighting between *Derg* soldiers and guerilla groups. While ordinarily Kossoyans were not severely affected by drought, the 1984-1985 famine was an exception. Feeding stations were set up in Ambaghiorgis, where even Taye, a person who was usually more than self-sufficient, joined in a grain distribution line.[25]

In Kossoye the process of rural *"encadrement"* reached its peak between 1986 and 1987 during the *Derg's* villagization campaign. Based on a similar campaign in Tanzania, this policy called for the reorganization of scattered households into planned urban settings. While the famine provided some rationale for resettling farmers from drought-stricken areas to more fertile regions in the south and west, the villagization campaign was entirely about control. It, too, involved resettlement, but rather than from one region to another, it was typically only for a distance of one or two kilometers (or even less), from a hamlet to a centrally planned village.[26]

Staff from the Ministry of Agriculture arrived in Kossoye sometime in 1986. One older man reported that the staff came from Dabat, Ambaghiorgis, and Gondar. "They were not people from this area. They were especially workers in the Ministry of Agriculture. They just destroy our homes in the daytime and go to their homes at night, via car."[27] New villages were laid out on grids in accordance with plans promulgated in Addis Ababa and enforced around the country, beginning in 1977-78 in Bale. As Clapham put it: "Villagization was…the most visible expression of the 'capture' of the peasantry, within residential perimeters accessible to wheeled transport, where they could be taxed, conscripted, and prevented from smuggling their produce to illegal open markets." When Clapham was taken on a tour of a reformed settlement by a local administrator, he observed that they "were clearly convinced that only in this way could the entrenched backwardness of the peasantry yield to the benefits of planned and centrally directed modernity."[28]

Kossoye's location made it a logical place for villagization. It was alongside the main road and a central access point to trails which led to the lowlands. It also had a school. The precise number of new residents who came to Kossoye as a result of villagization is not known, but interviews gathered since 1994 suggested that a total of about 50 new households settled in Cherema, Zinjero Wuha, and Gedeye. (See Map 4.) Approximately 30 resettled families came from Incheberet, about one kilometer away. Another 12 families came from Kifle, about a half-hour walk from town.[29] Most were Amhara, though some were Kemant who had relatives in Cherema.[30]

Map 4: Kossoye in 1994

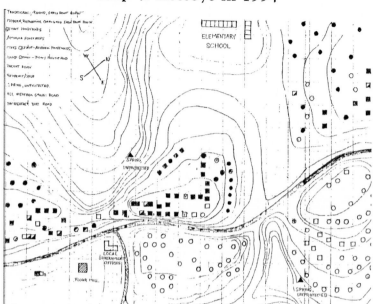

Source: This map was drawn by students from the University of Gondar
during a census and survey exercise in 1994.

Kassahun Belay Lemma was 57 years old in 1987 when
he was forced to move from Sisomedir, a hamlet about a
kilometer from the road. Although he had lived at various
times in the lowlands, he had been in Sisomedir since he was
11 years old. He recounted that the Ministry of Agriculture
used both force (*be gid*) and promises of better services to
move him into Cherema. When interviewed in 1994, he
said that he would like to move back but "now I am an old
man....There is nobody in the neighborhood there for me to
go back to."[31]

Taye's younger brother, Tagele, was a double loser as a
result of villagization. He had owned and farmed the land
where many of the new houses were built. Although the
Ministry of Agriculture workers promised compensation,
this pledge was not honored. More traumatic for Tagele

was that he was forced to destroy his house because it was large and made of stone—exceeding the lower standards for size and materials that had been set for the modern village. Tagele could not be convinced to dismantle his own home. As he explained: "I sweat to death to build that house. Even the wall around my house was built with stone, brought up from the hills, and it was above my chest and long. I had many bins (*goteras*) for storing cereals. I paid a worker 70 *birr* to help me build the house. I had 72 metal sheets. It was the best house in the area." When Tagele returned from three days in prison, he found his dwelling destroyed. His wife was so angry she became sick and did not talk for two years. Neighbors who had seen the house as a symbol of progress were confused.[32]

In theory villagization provided more efficient government, including delivery of health services, education, and agricultural extension projects. Villagization also gave the government in Addis Ababa an opportunity to extend its influence into rural communities—particularly since leadership of local governments (called Farmer's Associations, Peasant Associations, or *kebelles*) were drawn exclusively from the Ethiopian Worker's Party.

In many parts of Ethiopia people who experienced villagization returned to their old hamlets immediately after the fall of the *Derg* in 1991. People living in the Medhane Alem community followed this pattern, because villagization "was not accepted by the people. One thing, we were together in a marshy place. Another thing, there was no grazing area for the animals. And we were not happy, so when the *Derg* fell we immediately came back to our previous sites."[33]

But few people who were resettled in Kossoye town returned to their old homes, because the new town had advantages. Some had acquired plots that were better than they had before. Many had children who attended Kossoye school. Newer Kossoye residents also found opportunities for employment in local government and appreciated the moderately improved government services. As an old farmer put it: "Very few in number returned to their old places. The majority are here because it fits them. They have found it convenient to live here."[34]

Oppression and Resistance

The unpleasant side of the improved government service in Kossoye was greater government control. Recollecting the *Derg* provoked strong negative emotions in 1994 interviews. Kes Sisay recalled that members of the Worker's Party attempted to disrupt religious life, prohibiting the baptism of children, memorial feasts, and even church attendance. Some families waited until after the fall of the *Derg* to baptize their children. Others had their children baptized in the lowlands. When asked if he himself was persecuted by the *Derg*, Kes Sisay said: "No. They were afraid of us…if the *Derg* people killed an animal, they would deny that they did it."[35] This last statement suggests that the church retained some moral, if not political, authority through the hard years of the 1970s and 1980s.

People who worked for the government were perhaps most affected. A 39-year-old man who had been a policeman recalled that in 1985 he was fired after being accused of "not believing in party ideology."[36] When asked what he felt about teaching communist ideology, a 30-year-old teacher said: "I just teach it, if it is in the book, but I don't let it get in my mind."[37] Noting that there were thousands of *Derg* soldiers in the area between 1988 and 1991, the teacher went on to say that the *Derg* years were "a very difficult time. Every female who dresses [too well] was taken [to be] a prostitute. Even you can't speak anything to them. They didn't respect the community. We had many problems with them…no personal freedom, even to stay at your home."

Another teacher at the school recalled: "We were not allowed to talk in small groups. I was in a difficult situation. The Ministry of Education pays me my salary, but I was working practically for the Workers' Party. We were the ones who had to recruit children for military service. If you didn't [recruit students], you were accused by the *Derg*. We were the ones who did everything for the *Derg*. Teachers were the great victims of the *Derg*. They used them for whatever they wanted: villagization, recruitment...." The most traumatic event for the teacher, who wept after telling this story, happened when he was working at a neighboring school not far from Ambaghiorgis. One day party officials picked him up at his home in Gondar and took him by car to the school to recruit new soldiers. "After we finished the work, the party officials got in the car and drove back to Gondar, leaving me there with the parents. Then the community was about to kill me. I had to make a dead run for my life, running through the night...." [38]

Parents deeply resented the military for taking their sons while they were at school. Because of his own sad history helping Worker Party officials impress young students and perhaps also to protect himself from irate parents, this teacher told of warning students the "5 or 7 times" that soldiers came to the Kossoye school. "Usually whenever I saw the trucks [I]...ran to the classrooms and told the male students to disappear. Two times the soldiers tied me. With the help of the community I was released. I was beaten by sticks." The alarmed boys smashed closed classroom windows and ran down the escarpment, leaving the shocked and frightened girls behind to face the soldiers. [39] Subsequently fewer families sent their sons to the government schools, resulting in a remarkably lopsided ratio of girls to boys and a decline in male literacy. In 1994, 80% of all sixth graders were female. Over and over again, when asked why there were fewer boys than girls in school, people would cite fear of forced military service.

Despite their resistance, many boys and men found themselves in the military. The Chairman of the Farmer's Association, who was 29 years old when interviewed in 1994, was an appropriate age for military service but avoided conscription because "I was good at running and hiding." He reported that between 100 and 150 local boys and men went into the military and only 56 returned. He did not know how many died.[40] A teacher at the school estimated that at least 30 boys from the Kossoye school were killed, many only 12 or 13 years old at the time of their conscription.

Inevitably memories of the *Derg* came to be associated with a loss of family members. One young man recalled: "The *Derg* forced all of my older brothers to go to war. The one who helped me disappeared. The other came back, wounded, in 1986, and I take care of him now. The other one returned in 1991. They both live with me. My sister was married and has seven children and her husband was forced to go to war too. He returned alive, but is now unemployed. Also, they don't have pensions. I advised my sister to come to my home so that we can help each other."[41]

An older farmer lamented that one of his four sons "was forced into the military service, from grade 10, and I don't know whether he is dead or not. He has not returned."[42] When interviewed four years later, the same farmer said, with tears in his eyes: "My own boy was taken, out of the 10th grade, into the military and never returned."[43]

In January 1991 Kossoye became a battle site. The Ethiopian People's Revolutionary Democratic Front (EPRDF) guerillas came into the area sometime in 1989 or 1990. Whether they were Tigrayan or local people is unclear, but they were warmly received by the Kossoyans. They did not raze the town or kill people. They treated wives and daughters with respect. They were perceived by the villagers to be opposite from the *Derg* soldiers. At some point the EPRDF forces camped on the field in front of the school near where Haile Sellassie and Queen Elizabeth had stayed the night 26 years earlier. When *Derg* soldiers took up positions on the western side of the town, in order to block the EPRDF guerillas from driving into Gondar, the Kossoyans were caught in two days of modern warfare.

Many villagers escaped to the lowlands, but Taye and Tagele, then in their 70s, remained behind to protect their property. Tagele recalled: "The *Derg* soldiers stayed two kilometers from here and they were shelling us with BM rockets. It has a very deadly sound. Big rockets. I lost my home again and two of my sheep. And there were lots of houses here in Kossoye that were destroyed. No civilians were killed. But there were three EPRDF soldiers killed."

In the local version of the story, in order to spare the village, the EPRDF soldiers changed their position. As Tagele put it: "The EPRDF soldiers, for our sake, started to move in the other direction in order to stop the shelling [of the village]."[44]

The Revolution in Retrospect

There is no question that Kossoyans were relieved when the *Derg* Regime fell. Tagele said: "*Derg* means a curse from God. They are totally murderers. If you see Melaku Teferra in Gondar, he killed every student and child in the country. Everyone was his victims. Due to their murderous killings [students] went to America and Sudan. Even Taye's son fled, fearing Melaku's killing. There is no difference between adults or children, everyone fled. You cannot compare the *Derg* with the EPRDF. Mengistu has even killed his friends (General Teferi Banti, and Vice Chairman Atnafu Abate.) There is no comparison."[45]

People in Kossoye tended to distinguish between the revolution and the *Derg*. The literacy campaign was positive, while it lasted. The nationalization and redistribution of lands, although abused by local *Derg* government officials, benefited the Kemant, Falashas, and the poorest of the poor. The creation of the Farmers Association and other local institutions made government more accessible. On the other hand, Mengistu and his collaborators not only destroyed the prospect for civil discourse by eliminating opposition opinion, but they also put their country through the trauma of a long and bloody civil war. In Kossoye the war brought army raids for recruits at the local school, boys and men killed or maimed in battle, girls and women raped by *Derg* soldiers. The *Derg* also was associated with rigid ideologies, forced relocations, corrupt leaders, and unnecessary federal interference.

Kossoyans also saw the *Derg* years as a time of neglected social development. In the later 1980s, the protected spring in Zinjero Wuha fell into disrepair. The concrete structure with valves was broken and the pipe stolen. In its place people placed tree trunks and branches to keep out larger animals. The well provided a greatly reduced flow of unprotected water.

Education also suffered from the school being used as a military recruitment outpost. In Kossoye in 1967 there were 117 students, fairly evenly divided among males and females. Twenty four years later, in 1991, enrollment had increased to a grand total of 162 students, most of them female. The reluctance to send the boys to school lingered after the revolution. In 1996, only 25% of the elementary students were male and most of the fifth and sixth graders were female.

Villagization was also costly, emotionally and economically, especially for the people who had been forced to move into Kossoye. Most of the newcomers lived in a neighborhood called Gedeye and were Amhara. In a reversal on previous patterns of Kemant/Amhara relations, in 1994 the Kemant were better off. For example, 51% of Kemant lived in modern houses (rectangular design with corrugated iron roofs), and only 15% of the Amhara did so. Living in a modern house was also associated statistically with literacy.

In the 1994 survey, 40.7% of residents of modern houses were literate, while only 27% of grass roofed houses (*tukul*) residents were literate.[46] In general, a lower percentage of the Amhara families in Gedeye sent their children to school than did the Kemant families from Cherema and Zinjero Wuha.[47]

During the *Derg* years previous progress made in family planning slowed. As a result, annual rates of population increase rose to a disastrous 3%, with even higher rates reported in some areas south of Addis Ababa. By 1991 Ethiopia's population had risen to 45 million.

The *Derg* also had a negative effect on local leadership. For all his faults, Haile Sellassie was never the murderous despot that his immediate successor turned out to be. In Gondar the provincial aristocrat Colonel Tamirat Yigezu, considered by many to have been a good and progressive man, was eventually, after several appointees had held the post, replaced by Malaku Teferra, who developed a loathsome reputation as a tyrant. In Kossoye, relatively wealthy peasants were replaced by party members. Some of these individuals were competent and honest, but others abused their authority, took bribes for not sending sons to war, and appropriated the best land for themselves.

Local leaders had been relatively privileged men who had inherited land and who had earned or been awarded positions as *atbia dagna, chika shum,* or *shambel.* But they were also remembered as being honest and responsive. In reflecting on Taye's leadership, his brother-in-law said: "It was very good before Taye became old. Since then we have had corrupt officials. Everybody takes the money, even from the mill....The new leaders have no knowledge or wisdom of Ato Taye. When we elect Ato Taye, he controls everybody. Nobody can take away a single cent from the Farmer's Association. He wants each cent to be put in something important for the community. None of the other leaders has been so responsible. The other people after he became ill did not have the wisdom or character to lead."[48] A teacher who lived in town suggested the federal government influence undermined the effectiveness of the *chika shum's* successors: "The people in the Farmer's Association are not the ones you can depend on. Once in that position they can't ask questions; they have to take government orders. They are just executing the national government policy."[49]

Kossoyans traveled a great distance since the beginning of the revolution. In 1974 they were subjects of the last monarch of the great Solomonic dynasty and members of the Ethiopian Orthodox Church. In 1991, they were citizens in a modern political unit, connected through a socialist party organization to a multi-ethnic atheist state.

Notes

1. The following national narrative and analysis relies on Bahru Zewde, *A History of Modern Ethiopia*, Second Edition (Addis Ababa: Addis Ababa University Press, 2002), chapter 6; Donald Crummey, *Land and Society in the Christian Kingdom of Ethiopia From the Thirteenth to the Twentieth Century* (Urbana: University of Illinois Press, 2000), chapter 10; Paul Henze, *Layers of Time: A History of Ethiopia* (New York: Palgrave, 2000), chapters 9 and 10; Harold G. Marcus, *A History of Ethiopia* (Berkeley: University of California Press, 1994), chapters 13 and 14; and Christopher Clapham, "Controlling Space in Ethiopia," in *Remapping Ethiopia: Socialism & After*, ed. by Wendy James, Donald L. Donham, Eisei Jurimoto, Alessandro Triulzi, (Oxford: James Currey, 2002): 9-32.

2. Bahru, *A History of Modern Ethiopia*, 228-229.

3. Bahru Zewde, *Pioneers of Change in Ethiopia: The Reformist Intellectuals of the Early Twentieth Century* (Addis Ababa: Addis Ababa University Press, 2002), chapter 1.

4. Bahru, *A History of Modern Ethiopia*, 234.

5. Henze, *Layers of Time*, 332fn.

6. Clapham, "Controlling Space in Ethiopia," 14.

7. Interview 5, February 16, 1994.

8. Interview 5, February 16, 1994.

9. Bahru, *A History of Ethiopia*, 242.

10. Interview 11, February 1994.

11. Interview 22, February 1994.

12. Interview 28, February 21, 1994.

13. Interview 26, February 17, 1994.

14. Interview 2, February 15, 2006.

15. Interview 22, February 1994.

16. Interview 27, February 21, 1994.

17. Interview 28, February 21, 1994.

18. Interview 6, April 29, 1998.

19. Interview 21, February 19, 1994.

20. Interview 10, February 1994.

21. A farmer with usofructory rights can eat or sell whatever he grows on "his" land.

22. Interview 28, February 21, 1994.

23. Internal and external "Brain Drain" (more appropriately "Brain Hemorrhage") has continued to deplete Ethiopia's human resources, particularly in medicine and public health. Yoseph and Yohannes indicate that well over 50% of medical school graduates leave the country and do not return. It is also reported that many of the new health officers trained since 1996 are out-migrating, as are nurses. Yoseph A. Mengesha and Yohannes Kebede, "Brain Drain," in *Epidemiology and Ecology of Health and Disease in Ethiopia*, ed. by Yemane Berhane, Damen Haile Mariam, and Helmut Kloos (Addis Ababa: Shama Books, 2006), 308-324.

24. Clapham, "Controlling Space in Ethiopia," 20.

25. Interview 74, February 11, 2006.

26. An earlier and substantially more optimistic version of villagization in Kossoye is Andrew J. Carlson and Dennis G. Carlson, "Villagization in a Growing Ethiopian Town: Kossoge, 1963-1998," *Northeast African Studies*, Vol. 5, No. 2 (New Series) 1998: 117-133. On resettlement see Alula Pankhurst, "Surviving Resettlement in Wellegga: The Qeto Experience," in James et. al., *Remapping Ethiopia*, 133-150.

27. Interview 21, February 19, 1994.

28. Clapham, "Controlling Space in Ethiopia," 20.

29. Interview 5, February 13, 2006.

30. Interview 2, February 17, 1994.

31. Interview 12, February 1994.

32. Interview 21, February 18, 1994.

33. Interview 6, April 29, 1998.

34. Interview 2, May 1, 1998.

35. Interview 28, February 21, 1994.

36. Interview 6, February 1994.

37. Interview 13, February 1994.

38. Interview 27, February 21, 1994.

39. Interview 27, February 21, 1994.

40. Interview 17, February 1994.

41. Interview 26, February 1994.

42. Interview 22, February 1994.

43. Interview 48, May 1, 1998.

44. Interview 21, February 18, 1994.

45. Interview 21, February 18, 1994.

46. Carlson and Carlson, "Villagization in an Ethiopian Town," 117-133.

47. This may be related to their ethnic history, as Kemant families in Cherema and Zinjero Wuha felt a stronger need to compensate for minority status by material improvement and educational achievement.

48. Interview 22, February 1994.

49. Interview 13, February 1994.

1994: Women collecting water and washing clothes, near the old protected water source which had fallen into disrepair.

1994: Andrew, Dennis, and Anna Carlson at Taye's old eucalyptus plantation.

1994: The research group in Kossoye with Dennis Carlson, Steve Carlson, Mesganaw Fantahun, Mesfin Addisie, Asefash Gebru, Anna Carlson, Andrew Carlson, and Krista Magaw.

1994: Seated from left: Tagele Wubineh, Asefa Taye, Dennis Carlson, Taye Wubineh, Sisay Taye, and unidentified man.

1994: The kebele militia company.

1994: "Main Street" in Cherema.

CHAPTER SIX

AN ETHNIC DILEMMA

❖ ❖ ❖

After the fall of the *Derg* regime in 1991, the road north-east from Gondar was opened to civilian traffic. In 1992, 18 years after his last visit, Dennis Carlson returned to Kossoye for a happy and tearful reunion with old friends. In 1994, Andrew visited for ten days, accompanied by his wife, daughter, and brother. Students and faculty members from the Department of Environmental Health, now in the Gondar College of Medical Sciences, remapped the area and conducted a new census, as an earlier generation of students had done in 1965. Others in the research party conducted oral history interviews to learn the stories of life during the revolution, as well as reflections on the feudal era. Taye Wubineh rested at his home convalescing from a stroke, a shell of his former energetic self. A few hundred meters from the highway, at the Bata Mariam Church, Taye's oldest son, Kes Sisay, presided as head priest.

The transition government, led by the Ethiopian People's Revolutionary Democratic Front, took a more flexible view of national boundaries and ethnic identities than had the *Derg* regime.[1] In 1993, after nearly 30 years of war, Eritrea was allowed to secede, as had been agreed between the Eritrean and Tigrayan fronts before their joint campaign against the *Derg*. In 1995, after four years of transitional government, a constitution inaugurating the Federal Democratic

Republic of Ethiopia was approved. This provided Ethiopia with another kind of modern legal system and the apparatus of democratic government.[2] The country was divided into eleven regions, nine of these ethnic homelands, and the two others the cities of Addis Ababa and Dire Dawa. The ethnic federation was a clear departure from Amhara nationalism as the dominant political structure.

The new ethnic order created a Kemant dilemma. For centuries the Kemant had been contesting control of the Gondar region with the Amhara. The Kemant thought of themselves as the original inhabitants, along with other branches of the Agew peoples. Now Amhara nationalism had been rejected as the prevailing political paradigm, providing an opportunity for a Kemant revival. The problem was that the Kemant people remained in what was now designated the "Amhara region" of Ethiopia. Since Kemant assimilation into the Amhara Orthodox Christian culture was nearly complete—in what the anthropologist Frederick Gamst termed "terminal Amharicization" and the linguist Zelealim Leyew called "imminent language death"—the question became whether any cultural or political revival was possible.[3]

This drama had been playing out in the Amhara region for centuries, but especially since 1991. Most organizing activity was in the city of Gondar, described by Cressida Marcus in a 1999 essay as in a period of "imperial nostalgia" in which Christian Amhara engaged in religious restoration, focused especially on participation in church services and church construction.[4] In the Kossoye community a similar Christian restoration was taking place, marked by the building of two new churches (replacement for decrepit buildings) and a flurry of baptisms and memorial services. But there was also a parallel interest in a Kemant cultural revival in Gondar and its environs, including Kossoye, which involved renegotiating boundaries between the ethnic groups.

Ethnic Boundaries

At the very end of the *Derg* era, the Kossoye parish community had several ethnic groups. Tigrayans were few in number and usually married to Kemant or Amhara. The descendants of slaves intermarried with Kemant and Amhara and did not maintain separate cultural traditions. The five or six Bete Israel families lived in a distinct neighborhood and kept clear boundaries. About 150 Amhara families lived in the parish on the east side of the road, most in the neighborhood around Tsion Mariam Church. The largest group was the 550 Kemant families, living in the neighborhoods of Cherema, Zinjero Wuha, and Medhane Alem.[5]

In 1994 Kemant assimilation into the Amhara culture was more advanced than it had been in the 1960s. Virtually all were Orthodox Christians and Amharic speakers. Only a few older people retained any of the Kemantney language. Most Kemant sacred sites were neglected and the only leaders of Kemant traditional religion lived in Chilga and Aykel some 60 kilometers to the West, not far from Sudan.

Yet some boundaries that defined the Kemant as an ethnic group remained.[6] Kes Sisay reported in 1994 that he had conducted only two Kemant-Amhara weddings in 20 years.[7] For the most part, Amhara and Kemant lived in separate hamlets. Traditional Kemant believed they had "pure blood" and that their ancestors had been "white" or "pure" (*chewa*). This belief was often connected to the idea of Egyptian origins. Some Kemant also believed that members of their group were free of leprosy and other supposedly inherited diseases or disabilities (*komata* and *sentara*).[8] As one 29-year-old farmer put it, "in his blood and flesh, a Kemant is as clear as crystal clear water."[9] This sense of genetic superiority encouraged aspects of Kemant social separation.

Marriage to an Amhara might be thought to compromise the health of future generations, but in 1994 it was also increasingly socially acceptable. In interviews in which questions were posed about marriage, not a single Kemant said that they would not marry an Amhara, even when they preferred to marry a Kemant. The Community Health Worker who expressed the view that Kemant had "pure blood" had nevertheless been married three times, once to an Eritrean. "It was coincidental that [my] second and third wives were Kemant," he went on to say.[10] When a fifteen-year-old boy in the 9th grade was asked if he would marry a Kemant or Amhara, he responded: "Whatever I get."[11] However, he also expressed the view that "Amharas are not neat or clean." A fifteen-year-old girl in the 10th grade simply objected to the question of whether Orthodox Christians were Amhara or Kemant. "Everyone in the area is Amhara....The Kemant culture no longer matters."[12] The Amhara school teacher, who married a Kemant woman from Zinjero Wuha, said: "Nothing has affected me so far. Same religion. Almost same culture. Same language. I don't have any problems."[13]

Kes Eshete Bogale speculated in 1994 that the nationalization of land had affected marriage patterns. As he put it: "Until the *Derg* there was no marriage between Amhara and the Kemant. It is because of the land. The Amhara say, 'We are landlords.' The Kemant have no land. But since the *Derg* proclamation about land, there is no problem about land. Land has become 'of all.' So there are now many marriages between groups."[14] Tagele Wubineh had a similar impression: "Previously Amhara didn't want marriage, because they did not want Kemant to inherit their land. They thought that Kemant were fools. Meanwhile, Kemant thought they had the 'pure blood,' and the Amharas didn't."[15]

Continuing ethnic boundaries could be seen in patterns of church affiliation. The oldest church in the area, Tsion Mariam, had an entirely Amhara congregation. The newest of the highland churches, Medhane Alem, had an entirely Kemant congregation. Kes Sisay's Bata Mariam Church had a congregation that was evenly divided between Amhara and

Kemant.[16] It is notable that while his father always attended Medhane Alem, Sisay became head priest of the mixed church. Kes Eshete Bogale said: "Now things are changing. People are going to churches that are closer to where they live. Even if the father goes to one church, the son will go to another."[17]

For Amharas some social boundaries remained, especially in Kemant neighborhoods. When an Amhara teacher who lived in Cherema and married a Kemant was asked what would happen if he went to the Medhane Alem church, he responded: "No Amhara will go to Medhane Alem Church on purpose." Then he was asked, "What happens if you go in?" His response: "No problem. It is just that the Amhara don't want to go."[18] Of the three churches, Amhara and Kemant were expected to worship together only in Bata Mariam.

Not everyone in Kossoye was an active member in one of the Orthodox Christian churches. Some people were nominally Christian but did not attend church, possibly motivated by financial considerations, since church attendance required payment of fees. Kes Sisay noted that some people attempted to avoid the fees by attending a church outside their neighborhood, telling the priest that they had paid at the home church. The priests organized themselves to prevent this kind of cheating and said that people had to worship where they paid their fees.[19]

Among the educated young people who had moved to Gondar and then returned was a small group of Pentecostals (*Pentes*), most under 30 years of age. Kes Sisay compared the Pentecostal movement to "an epidemic in the schools in Gondar. Foreigners came to Gondar and taught. Young people came to the countryside (Kossoye, Dabat, Debre Tabor). The worst problem was that they said 'Mary was just like any woman.'"[20] The children of two local priests were told that they could not be buried in the church cemetery if they stayed with the Pentecostals.

Occasionally a Muslim family would settle in the new town, usually renting a house along the road and working as a weaver or tailor. For religious services they would have to attend one of two mosques in Gondar, where there were perhaps 20,000 Muslims. In Kossoye Muslims kept a low profile.

The most obvious non-Christian group was the Ethiopian Jews (known as the Bete Israel or, pejoratively, as the Falashas). Their neighborhood was across the road from Cherema and Zinjero Wuha. They worshipped in one of their homes since they did not have a synagogue or a rabbi. On religious holidays they could go to Wolleka, on the outskirts of Gondar, where there was a large Bete Israel community. On occasion the Bete Israel might drink beer *(tella)* with Kemant or Amhara, but in principle they did not eat together or marry. Strong ethnic boundaries remained.

In sum, despite efforts by the *Derg* to reduce the influence of the Ethiopian Orthodox Church, it remained the dominant institution in Kossoye. Kemant assimilation into Amhara Christian culture had continued, perhaps even accelerated, but not to the point of eliminating ethnic boundaries. Jews, Muslims, and Pentecostals lived in the area but were at the margins of the majority community.

"Exodus" of the Bete Israel

The fall of the *Derg* government set in motion a series of changes in ethnic relations and boundaries that caused disruption in Kossoye. Beginning in the late 1980s the Israeli government and American Jewish organizations became concerned about the welfare of the Ethiopian Jews (Bete Israel). American Jews funded missions staffed by expatriate health professionals to monitor the situation for the Bete Israel, especially in the Gondar area. This ultimately set in motion negotiations between the Israeli and Mengistu governments for the exodus of the Bete Israel. In 1990 and 1991 about 25,000 Bete Israel were allowed to leave Ethiopia, allegedly accompanied by a payment of $35 million USD to Ethiopian government officials.[21]

This exodus was a major disruption in Kossoye. Despite their small numbers and the social distance between Bete Israel and other groups, the Kemant and Bete Israel felt they were cultural cousins and shared a sense of solidarity against the Amharas.[22] The larger Kossoye community relied on the Bete Israel to make pottery and tools. And there were friendships. An Amhara teacher who lived in Cherema and married into a local Kemant family said: "I felt very, very sad when they left because we used to have very good times with them."[23] Kes Sisay recalled that he was sorry when the Bete Israel left. He accompanied them to Gondar, to show the honor and respect he felt for them. His uncle, Tagele Wubineh, said: "We felt very sad. We thought it was Satan's work; maybe God is angry with them. It is not a normal thing for people (elderly, pregnant) to leave their homeland."[24] Kes Eshete Bogale also expressed sadness, noting that he had received letters and gifts from old friends who were now in Israel. He was also sure that "the Falashas have a better life in Israel."[25]

Some Kossoyans were confused about why the Bete Israel left. Emahoy Alsegid Bizuneh, a 52-year-old nun, put it this way: "They were living separately over there. We don't have many relations with them. I don't worry much about them. It is their business. I don't know whether they went to a foreigner's country or to the sky." She was then asked, "Don't you know they went to Israel?" Her response: "I heard that but I don't know whether that is their original country or not....They told us that they were going to 'our country.' I didn't know whether to believe them or not....They are a different group. It is not my business to ask why."[26]

Kes Sisay recalled that "some Falashas asked to be baptized in order to stay in Kossoye." But they were discouraged from converting to Christianity because "no one would marry their children."[27] In fact, marriages of Bete Israel with Kemant and Amharas did occur, after Bete Israel converted to Christianity,[28] but the boundaries separating Bete Israel from the Orthodox Christians were strong. For Kemant, it was acceptable to speak of marriage with Amhara while it was not acceptable to speak of marriage with Bete Israel, even if it was practiced. Kemant attended celebrations and funerals of Amhara but not of the Bete Israel.

Of course rules are broken. One Kemant man interviewed in 1994, whose story is told earlier, was severely burdened by family obligations and lack of land. He found a way of surviving by divorcing his wife and marrying a Bete Israel woman. This crossing of group boundaries through marriage allowed him to go to Israel, where it is reported he now serves in the military.[29]

It does not seem that the Bete Israel were persecuted, at least not in Kossoye, but they certainly were made to feel alien. Amhara and Kemant children often expressed fear of Bete Israel children, accusing them of having the evil eye (*buda*). A fifteen-year-old Kemant boy who had Bete Israel friends admitted believing "the Falashas had bad spirits (*buda*)."[30] Most adults did not encourage this talk. As an Amhara teacher at the school put it: "We used to say, if the Falashas have the evil spirit, why don't they affect the teachers? We also used to take students to Falasha village to see handicrafts."[31]

More generally the argument can be made that the Bete Israel were making advances in the years before their exodus. Under Haile Sellassie, Ethiopian Jews had not owned land or worked as farmers; they made their living as potters and blacksmiths, an artisan class. As a result of the revolution, however, Bete Israel access to land improved and at the very least allowed diversification of their family economies.[32]

The Kemant Revival

In 1994 an extension agent from the Ministry of Agriculture described the Kemant in Kossoye parish as being "completely swallowed by Amhara culture."[33] Kes Sisay reported that the three Orthodox Christian churches had more than 70 priests and 700 families, for a total of 3,000 to 6,000 people. Bata Mariam had 10 priests and 100 families; Tsion Mariam ten priests and 100 families; and Medhane Alem had 50 priests and 500 families.[34] If one took a broad view of church functions, at some point perhaps 10% of all adults in the community served some role in the church as priests, deacons, students, nuns, or monks. Moreover, the majority of the community participated in Sunday and other holiday services. There is no question that the dominant institution in Kossoye was (in 1994 and still in 2008) the Ethiopian Orthodox Church.

Although the *Derg* confiscated some church property, the churches in Kossoye retained most of their possessions and influence. Bata Mariam and Tsion Mariam lost land, the former having only ten *tind*.[35] For some reason—perhaps because it was an entirely Kemant congregation and some distance from the main road—Medhane Alem retained control of 20 hectares of land and a valuable forest of eucalyptus trees.[36] When these trees were sold at the end of the *Derg* era, the 450,000 EB profit went to the parish community, not to the government. These funds were divided between the three highland churches. Medhane Alem and Bata Mariam constructed large rectangular concrete structures designed by a church architect in Gondar. Tsion Mariam could only afford renovations. These were by far the costliest capital expenditures ever undertaken in the parish and served as a monument to the churches' continuing power and influence.

After 1991, people in the Gondar region and Kossoye experienced a Kemant revival. The leader of the Kemant movement in the Gondar area was Nega Gete, a health officer who owned a pharmacy. Nega began organizing in early 1991, bringing to the cause a sense of personal destiny. As a boy growing up in the lowland area of Tikil Dingaye, about 40 kilometers due north from Gondar, Nega had strong relationships with his father and grandfather, both Kemant. His grandfather offered him a number of prophecies: "You will not be a peasant. You will be a doctor [*hakim*]....He said the people of Kemant will be gathered in the center of Gondar in the future. Then the whole society of the Kemant will lead the place as a head."[37] In other words, Nega's grandfather envisioned a Kemant restoration to power in the Gondar region.

When Nega graduated from the Haile Sellasie I Public Health College as a health officer, he remembered his grandfather's predictions. Subsequently he interviewed older people who retained a memory of Kemant and Agew cultures and learned Kemant place names for much of the Amharized Gondar region. In the process he developed a sense that the Gondar region in fact had been "Kemantland."[38]

Nega also recalled his grandfather's prophecies of a large Kemant gathering in Gondar, which he took as his reason to organize. "I just propagate the idea that we are an ethnic people who assimilated and lost our language," he recalled in 1998. "We have to organize and use fertile ground now. The existing government is providing an autonomous self-governing system. We have to be organized and develop our area culturally as well as economically and be political participants." Nega noted that the Humera Agew, with a recorded population of 143,000 people (less than the 172,000 Kemant recorded in the 1994 census), had achieved self-government and "are getting a chance to learn their language in school."[39]

In 1993 Nega came to Kossoye to speak about the Kemant revival. It seems the meeting was held at the Bata

Mariam Church, perhaps at *senbete*, since both Amhara and Kemant reported being present. (The meeting might also have occurred in front of the Farmer's Association building.) An Amhara teacher married to a local Kemant woman recalled: "I was there at [the] meeting—when Ato Nega began to speak—people started to split, Amhara from Kemant. This man did nothing for the community. It is just for…personal reasons. I am very angry with him."[40] The Chairman of the Kebele, a 29-year-old farmer who was Kemant by ancestry, opposed Nega's cultural restoration efforts. As he put it, "because we lost all our culture and language it is difficult to have an organization."[41]

After the meeting a discussion ensued about the ethnic ownership of the Bata Mariam Church, the only church in the parish that included Kemant and Amhara people. For a while, relations between the groups deteriorated, but Kes Sisay "called on everybody and said that Bata belongs to all of us."[42]

There are different perspectives on what happened next. Nega said the resistance to the revival movement did not come from the rural Kemant communities but rather from the urban, educated people and the Amhara. "I can say that the whole Kemant are with me….The Amhara government was afraid of the organization of the Kemant. I don't know why. I guess they claim this is the Amhara area, this region, and the Amhara society claims Gondar from surrounding Agew peoples….I was advocating with the Kemant to get ethnic rights from the Amhara."[43] The Amhara did have reasons to feel threatened. If Nega's application to the Federal government had been successful, Amhara would have had to share power and resources in a region that they considered their homeland.

Many people in the parish had no interest in a Kemant revival. This obviously included the Amhara but also many people of Kemant ancestry like Tagele Wubineh. He said: "We have lost our language and there is nothing to organize for."[44] Another old man, Teshome, was also resigned: "We have no choice except to be Amhara. When I was younger the older ones tried very hard to teach us Kemantney. But we neglected them and treated them with contempt. Now we are sorry. There is no one who knows about Kemant to teach our children. Now it is too late. We must be Amhara."[45]

Yet the idea of a Kemant revival did appeal to some. A 29-year-old farmer with a sixth-grade education whose father had refused to teach any of his children Kemantney because of all the difficulties he had experienced said: "I will try and am eager to know the language, and put a high priority on this."[46] A 31-year-old farmer who had learned to read in the literacy campaign said that the government should print books in the language, so he could study.[47] The 39-year-old Community Health Worker spoke of his plans to learn Kemantney and teach it to his 5 children: We "must restore language because [it was] destroyed by Amhara. Feudal powers were controlling. Amhara forced our ancestors that unless [they] accept Christianity, they wouldn't get flat land. [They were] pushed to the cliffs."[48]

Among the younger generation, especially those in school, it seems that there was little desire to revive Kemant culture. A 15-year-old male in 9th grade in Ambaghiorgis admitted Kemant ancestry and noted that his grandmother spoke the language and that "sometimes I can speak Kemant." He had visited the Kemant sacred place (Jigeru) many times, mostly to cut wood, and had also witnessed two sacrifices to bring rain, an ox in 1991 and a sheep in 1993. He expressed hostility to the Bete Israel, saying the evil eye is gone now that the Falashas have returned to Israel, and also to Amhara, because they "are not neat or clean." Despite this sense of group identity and exposure to Kemant culture, however, in his view "Kemant has no meaning."[49]

Although nobody advocated revival of the Kemant religion, there seems to have been some renewed interest in sacred spaces and traditions. One of the longest standing

Kemant traditions that continued to be practiced in the early 1990s was a ceremony conducted in the woods on the hilltop on December 3, at which time Kemant gathered to slaughter a white calf. During his childhood in the 1930s and 1940s, an old farmer said that "everything stopped" for the celebration.[50] It is not clear who organized the ceremonies in 1991 and 1993, but they appear to have attracted large crowds.

In the early 1990s, priests noted increased traffic to the remaining Kemant sacred sites. The newest of the parish churches, St. Michael, was built on an old Kemant sacred site known as Degena. This was a strategy the Orthodox Christian Church had used often to co-opt the allure of the Kemant religion. Another site, Abi Nora, on a bluff looking over the escarpment, had lost its appeal and power because *Derg* soldiers had camped in the place and cut its trees. A third site, Endorit, was reported to be "no longer in use." Kes Sisay noted that "even now, those who are Christians go to these places and slay sheep and so on."[51]

The one sacred site that retained its attraction and power was Jigeru. When the Carlsons visited it in 1994 they found well-worn paths and recent fires, indicating continuing usage and sacrifices. Moreover, one of the only remaining Kemant speakers in town, a farmer in his seventies, and several shepherds, were happy to show the way, demonstrating familiarity with the place. The old farmer bowed and prayed in Kemantinay at the grove, without shame, in front of the foreign visitors and the shepherds.[52] The Carlsons were warned by the shepherds not to wander into the woods, because snakes and spirits lived there.

There was disagreement about how any place became sacred. According to the Wambar, the major Kemant religious leader: "To make one place a sacred or holy place, first it should be on a mountain: the first thing. Then, one father will start it. Since that place is taken as a holy place, we will keep the place clean. For example, women will not come to that place during menstruation....We pray. We sacrifice. We sacrifice sheep, oxen, cows, not goats." He went on to say that it was not the trees or the place that Kemant prayed to: "When we practice our religion, we believe God will hear our prayers, but we also have three angels, like the Christians, who can listen and forward our requests to God."[53] The three angels—Jakaranda, Kebirwuha, and Megzana—conveyed prayers to God.

Local beliefs included more mystery and power. The local traditional healer, who worked for a time as the Community Health Worker, said: "[one] must be cautious [going into the grove]. Not as you like. Can be sick and die. Spirits [*kole*] may cause sickness or death. Also tree leaves may be dangerous. For [avoiding] mental illness have to go at 3 AM—then pray before cutting leaves. Hold leaf, pray, then cut leaf. Otherwise maybe go mad yourself."[54] As Teshome put it: "Every year before, Kemant used to sacrifice cows, oxen, sheep on Jigeru. Now it is only hens. Now he will go by himself with his hen and slay it, blessing in the name of God the Father, the Son, the Holy Ghost, because now he does not know Kemant language or prayer. Now he is a Christian and knows Christian prayer. Why does he do it? Only to keep his wife, children, and wealth safe."[55] The last remaining Kemant speaker in Kossoye, Adungna Ewentis, expressed a similarly Christian perspective on Kemant religion when he said that he wanted three Orthodox Christian churches built in the Sacred Grove: one for Amhara, one for Tigray, and one for the Kemant.[56]

The Christianization of Kemant religious practice in the Kossoye area required some vigilance on the part of the clergy. Kes Sisay discouraged any recognition of the Kemant religion. "We order them to pray [and] fast if they go there," he said in 1994. He also said that he threatened to withhold blessings from people who visited the Jigeru, because "the Bible forbids [going to the grove], God forbids, the 10 Commandments forbid."[57] When Andrew Carlson noted that he himself had been to Jigeru with Adungna, Kes Sisay said: "I don't think he is going there. The priests observe and follow those who do."

The implications of a Kemant revival were troubling for Kes Sisay. On the one hand he said: "I am sad no longer to speak [Kemantney]."[58] But he simply could not reconcile the language with the Kemant religion and his loyalty to the Ethiopian Orthodox Church. He was the first person in his family to become a priest, the result of extensive education and sacrifice. He was the chief leader (*aleka*), the auditor, and teacher in a congregation with both Amhara and Kemant parishioners. He was in the midst of a building campaign on a new concrete church, a project which by the time of completion will have taken nearly twenty years. As leader of a church with both Kemant and Amhara parishioners, he had an interest in discouraging ethnic conflict which might have arisen as a result of a Kemant cultural revival.[59]

Culture Death

In the middle 1960s, the anthropologist Frederick C. Gamst spent 14 months in the Gondar area investigating Kemant culture. He camped in Aykel outside the compound of the Wambar, Muluneh Mersha, the spiritual and political leader of one moiety (kinship network) of the Kemant people, learning what remained of this "ancient pagan Hebraic culture." The other moiety in Kerker, in the lowlands below Kossoye, no longer had a Wambar. Gamst's research led him to conclude that the Kemant culture had reached a point of "terminal Amharization." "The Kemant way of life cannot be greatly prolonged…because the Kemant sociocultural system is no longer truly viable."[60]

In 1998, more than thirty years after Gamst wrote those words, Andrew Carlson visited the Wambar in Aykel. About 75 years old, the Wambar remained robust. He continued to attract attention, from Graham Hancock, who wrote about him in his popular inquiry into the ark of the covenant, *The Sign and the Seal,* and from Zelealem Leyew, who was researching a dissertation on the linguistic status of the Kemant language.[61] The Kemant organizer, Nega Gete, had established contact with him. The Wambar encouraged interest in his language, culture, and history.[62]

It might be argued that the Wambar's continued vitality refuted Gamst's predictions. After all, how long can a culture remain in a terminal state? As Andrew walked through Aykel with the Wambar, villagers bowed and showed the old man great respect. The Wambar said that the Kemant still had 25 priests, 15 prayer sites, and about 1000 followers. Most were over 50 years of age, but a few were under 30. The Wambar's second son, then 22 years old and already a priest, had been named as his successor and had begun his clerical education.[63]

Nevertheless, it was clear that Gamst was essentially correct about the viability of the Kemant sociocultural system. Even in the Wambar's community on the outskirts of Aykel, neighbors displayed Christian crosses on top of their houses, an uncommon signification of Christianity which might also be construed as a rebuke of the Wambar's authority. More important, all the Wambar's daughters had married Christians, and even his wife wore a Christian cross. He noted that his sons-in-law had previously been traditional Kemant, but now all were Christian, including, of course, the grandchildren. "This is something that is out of my control," he said. "It is their choice."[64]

Later that month Andrew visited Zelealem Leyew, a linguist at Addis Ababa University. Zelealem noted that the 1994 census found only 1600 bilingual speakers of Kemantney among a population of about 200,000 ethnic Kemant, mostly in the Gondar region. He went on to say that the youngest bilingual Kemant speaker found in his linguistic research was 37 years old and lived in a remote valley 4 hours' walk from Aykel. Most important, "there are no monolingual speakers." "So the life expectancy of the language is not long," Zelealem concluded.[65]

Given the federal government's recognition of ethnic groups, it is understandable that a number of Kemant in Kossoye and elsewhere considered Zelealem's work a positive sign that something might be done for the revival of the language. Nega Gete talked about starting a school, building upon the foundation of Zelealem's research. Others in Kossoye mentioned the possibility that the government would publish texts in Kemantney, thus making it possible for them to study the language.

But the obstacles to language revival were many. Zelealem eloquently explained that "for a revival of a language to happen one needs more than just willingness of the people. It is true people would like a school. But should we get support from the government? Should we get trained teachers of the language? I am willing to teach the grammar. But as far as I know, children in school never want to be considered Kemant. They are the potential of the future of the language. But can the attitude be changed? We would have to see many things come together. I think it is a good idea. But does the economy of the country allow this? We are undertaking elementary mother tongue learning, but it takes a lot of money, books."[66]

In Kossoye the most logical institution to revive Kemant language would be the public school, but there have been no initiatives to introduce teaching any languages except Amharic and English. In some regions in Ethiopia ethnic languages are taught. In Tigray all public school instruction happens in English and Tigrayan. In Oromia strong efforts are made to teach Oromifa as well as Amharic and English. Afar groups have lobbied for teaching their languages in schools. But similar initiatives to teach Kemantney in Gondar area public schools have not gone far. Although teachers of Kemant ethnicity are attracted to job assignments in the Kossoye school, and though they may express pride in Kemant culture, their education has been entirely in Amharic and English. If there were a Kemantney language program—texts and teachers—there would probably be interest on the part of more teachers. But more important to the children and to most parents in the community are opportunities for advancement, which typically means mastering Amharic and English. The difficulty the school has in maintaining the most rudimentary library in English and Amharic suggests the problem for Kemantney language restoration, even if there were books.

Kemant religious revival might be less difficult. The next Wambar is not a fluent Kemantney speaker. Christianized Kemant have continued to visit sacred sites and maintain some memory of traditional practices. In Aykel the Wambar and his son continue to practice their religion, praying before groups that include Christianized Kemant who stand and eat apart from non-Christianized Kemant.

There is no question, however, that Kemant culture is not in ascendancy. In 2006, Andrew Carlson found Nega Gete resigned to the fact that there would be no revival of the Kemant religion and no special recognition for the Kemant. Nega's book on Kemant history had attracted some attention in Gondar, notably negative reviews from the Ethiopian Orthodox Church which contested his charge that Orthodox Christianity had forcibly assimilated the Kemant. Nega challenged the negative reviews before the archbishop; as a result he was offered a financial settlement, and priests in the region were instructed not to speak ill of him.[67]

Meanwhile, in 2006 the elderly Wambar was bogged down in another lawsuit about Kemant sacred sites. He had charged the Ethiopian Orthodox Church with violating an agreement made in the 1950s to share land that had been Kemant. The Ethiopian Orthodox Church, it seems, pushed out the Kemant by marking the territory with buildings and fences. In this lawsuit, the court ruled in favor of the Ethiopian Orthodox Church's right to build a new building, leaving the Wambar with one less sacred site in the Aykel area.

In Kossoye, there are no longer Kemant priests or even Kemant speakers. The last of the sacred sites, Jigeru, is neglected and eucalyptus trees encroach on the stand of indigenous trees, including olive and oak, while cattle wander through the forest, followed by young shepherds who no longer seem intimidated by rumors of spirits in the trees. There is no evidence of recent sacrifices. In Kossoye the Kemant ethnic dilemma—whether to try to restore the old culture or accept Amharization—has lost its significance.

Notes

1. Histories of Ethiopia generally do not cover the years since the fall of the Derg. An exception is Paul B. Henze's *Layers of Time: A History of Ethiopia* (New York: Palsgrove, 2001), which offers a review of the period between 1991 and 1998. Other studies include: Sarah Vaughan and Kjetil Tronvoll, *The Culture of Power in Contemporary Ethiopian Political Life* (Stockholm: Sida Studies No. 10, 2005); Abebe Zegeye and Sigfried Pausewang, eds. *Ethiopia: in Change: Peasantry, Nationalism and Democracy* (London: British Academic Press, 1994); Bahru Zewde and Siegfried Pausewang, eds., *Ethiopia: The Challenge of Democracy from Below* (Uppsala: Nordiska Afrikainstituet; Addis Ababa: Forum for Social Studies, 2002); and a collection of papers in Wendy James, Donald Donham, Eisei Kurimoto, Alessandro Triulzi, editors, *Remapping Ethiopia: Socialism and After* (Oxford: James Currey, 2002).

2. The 1955 Constitution created the first modern legal system.

3. Frederick C. Gamst, *The Qemant: A Pagan-Hebraic peasantry of Ethiopia* (Prospect Heights, Illinois: Waveland Press, Inc., 1984 reissue of 1969 printing), 122; Zelealem Leyew, *The Kemantney Language: A Sociolinguistic and Grammatical Study of Language Replacement* (Koln: Rudiger Koppe Verlag, 2003).

4. Cressida Marcus, "Imperial Nostalgia: Christian Restoration & Civic Decay in Gondar," in *Remapping Ethiopia: Socialism & After*, Wendy James, et al., eds., (Oxford: James Currey, 2002), 239-256.

5.   This is based on Kes Sisay's estimate of the number of families in each of the three churches.

6.   On ethnic boundaries in Southern Ethiopia see Karl-Eric Knutsson, "Dichotomization and Integration," in *Ethnic Groups and Boundaries: The Social Organization of Culture Difference*, Fredrik Barth, ed., (Long Grove, Illinois: Waveland Press, Inc, 1998 reissue of 1969 edition), 86-100.

7.   Interview 28, February 21, 1994.

8.   Interview 6, February 16, 1994.

9.   Interview 30, February 18, 1994.

10.   Interview 6, February 16, 1994.

11.   Interview 7, February 16, 1994.

12.   Interview 24, February 19, 1994.

13.   Interview 13, February 1994.

14.   Interview 52, April 29, 1998.

15.   Interview 21, February 18, 1994.

16.   Interview 28, February 21, 1994.

17.   Interview 10, February 17, 1994.

18.   Interview 13, February 17, 1994.

19.   Interview 47, April 29, 1998.

20.   Interview 28, February 21, 1994.

21.   Henze, *Layers of Time: A History of Ethiopia*, 325-327.

22.   Interview 10, February 1994.

23.   Interview 13, February 1994.

24.   Interview 21, February 18, 1994.

25.   Interview 10, February 16, 1994.

26.   Interview 4, February 17, 1994.

27.   Interview 28, February 21, 1994.

28. An example of this is the Bete Israel woman who was serving as a cook in the army when the people in Wolleka left. She bemoaned her fate but ended up converting to the Orthodox Christian Church and marrying an Amhara. Later she renounced her marriage and made her way to Israel. Interviews 1 and 2, February 24, 1994.

29. Interview 61, January 4, 2005.

30. Interview 7, February 16, 1994.

31. Interview 13, February 17, 1994.

32. Interview 10, February 16, 1994.

33. Interview 8, February 20, 1994.

34. Interview 47, April 29, 1998.

35. Interview 28, February 21, 1994.

36. Interview 52, April 29, 1998.

37. Interview 55, April 23, 1998.

38. Interview 52, April 29, 1998. In Nega Gete's words: "I went to Gondar and asked old people where Kerker is. They tell me that Kerker is Gondar. The Angerib River and the Kaha River demark land that is Kerker. There is also another river (Magedge) which starts near Kossoye and goes below that mountain (the area is known as Wollage). Beyond that is the Demazza River, that goes through Azezo. The lands between these rivers are Kemant lands."

39. Interview 52, April 29, 1998.

40. Interview 13, February 17, 1994.

41. Interview 17, February 18, 1994.

42. Interview 13, February 17, 1994.

43. Interview 52, April 29, 1998.

44. Interview 21, February 18, 1994.

45. Interview 22, February 18, 1994.

46. Interview 26, February 17, 1994.

47. Interview 5, February 16, 1994.

48. Interview 6, February 16, 1994.

49. Interview 7, February 16, 1994.

50. Interview 21, February 18, 1994. The December 3 ritual is mentioned by several individuals, including Interview 30, February 18, 1994.

51. Interview 47, April 29, 1998.

52. Interview 3, February 18, 1994.

53. Interview 56, in Aykel with the Wambar, Muluneh Mersha, April 24-26, 1998.

54. Interview 6, February 16, 1994.

55. Interview 48, May 1, 1998.

56. Interview 3, February 18, 1994.

57. Interview 28, February 21, 1994.

58. Interview 28, February 21, 1994.

59. Interview 47, April 29, 1998.

60. Frederick C. Gamst, *The Qemant: A Pagan-Hebraic Peasantry of Ethiopia*, 122.

61. Graham Hancock, *The Sign and the Seal: A Quest for the Lost Ark of the Covenant* (New York: Touchstone, 1992), 241-247; Zelealem Leyew, *The Kemantney Language*.

62. "We like you," the Wambar said to Andrew. "We want people like you to study our language, our culture, our history." Interview 56, with Wambar Muluneh Mersha, April 24, 1998.

63. Interview 56, with Wambar Muluneh Mersha, April 24, 1998.

64. Interview 56, with Wambar Muluneh Mersha, April 24, 1998.

65. Interview 57, May 2, 1998.

66. Interview 57, May 2, 1998.

67. Interview 81, May 13, 2006.

2005: Kes Sisay preaching at the Bata Mariam Church. The new concrete building was constructed using profits from the Medhane Alem eucalyptus forest.

1998: The Kemant Wambar (center) with his son (left) and a senior priest (right). The son has been chosen to be the next Wambar.

157

1994: Beulah Downing with the last of
Kossoye's Kemant speakers in the sacred grove,
Jigeru.

1994: View northeast from Jigeru into the
lowlands.

CHAPTER SEVEN

LAND AND POPULATION

❖ ❖ ❖

Early in 1998 while in Gondar on other business, Dennis Carlson visited Kossoye for an afternoon. He knew Taye Wubineh had been paralyzed by a stroke but not that he had died or that he had arrived on the day of Taye's memorial service (*teskar*), conducted one year after his death. In the Amhara tradition the *teskar* is an occasion for feasting and remembering. The occasion often draws many people, depending on the status and wealth of the deceased. Taye's *teskar* was unusually large. Six oxen were slaughtered. Hundreds of relatives, neighbors, and friends attended. Despite confiscation of some of his property in the revolution, he had remained, by local standards, a "rich man" (*habtam*). He had held a number of public offices, first under Haile Sellassie, then under the *Derg*. Despite the fact that he never learned to read and write, and despite the tremendous drain of war and revolution, Taye had been an innovator working for a more modern Ethiopia. He demonstrated leadership and commitment to his community.

Though Taye was interested in Dennis Carlson's ideas, he ultimately was not convinced about the need for family planning. Even though his wife received an intrauterine contraceptive device in 1967, she had it removed shortly thereafter and continued becoming pregnant. By the time she reached menopause she had delivered 11 live births. Taye's oldest son, Sisay, fathered 12 children. That all but one of Sisay's children survived into adulthood is evidence of the modern health attitudes and practices that made Taye so instrumental in improving health in the Kossoye community. The size of these families, however, reflects more traditional ideas about procreation.

The health transition that Taye helped implement in Kossoye, beginning in 1963 with the building of the protected spring, was having negative consequences by the 1990s. The reason was that population growth had exceeded available land. Families could no longer assume that their sons and daughters would be able to subsist as farmers. Food was in short supply, and more people than ever went hungry. This was not Taye's responsibility, of course. The population and nutrition crises in Kossoye were indicative of national and global trends.[1]

Population Growth

Through the 1970s and 1980s, the Family Guidance Association of Ethiopia (FGAE) continued providing services and training personnel as it had since the last years of Haile Sellassie's government. The *Derg* government maintained participation in United Nations organizations and sent official representatives to the global conference sponsored by WHO and UNICEF in Alma Ata, Soviet Union, in 1978. The theme was "Health for All by the Year 2000," a broad-based slogan with political and social implications as well as technical health objectives, including universal access to family planning services.[2] Ethiopia immediately signed the Accord, and in 1980 the Ministry of Health changed the name of the Department of Maternal and Child Health to the Department of Maternal and Child Health/Family Planning, an indication of the government's intention to incorporate the Declaration of Alma Ata into Ethiopian health policies and programs. Nevertheless, during the *Derg* era, from 1974 until 1991, little attention and few resources were committed to family planning.

The population growth rate in Ethiopia began to accelerate slowly in the first half of the 20th century, as in other peasant societies around the world: 1.8% per year by 1950, 2.1% by 1960, 2.4% by 1970, and 2.6% by 1980.[3] The census of 1984 revealed that the rate of population growth continued to accelerate, with a population of 42 million people and an annual growth rate of 2.9 %.[4] The rate in the Gondar region was even higher: 3.3%.[5] The World Bank estimated that the period from 1987 to 2000 showed a national annual rate of growth of 3.1%. One study in the Harar region showed the annual rate to have reached 5%.[6] Obviously, few women in Ethiopia were using modern contraceptive methods. In rural areas the national contraceptive prevalence rate (CPR) was estimated to be 2% in 1980 and had only increased to 4% by 1990, though in Addis Ababa rates ranged from 17 to 35%.[7] In a four-year study from 1987 until 1990 in Butajira in central Ethiopia, Desta Shamebo found the CPR was only 2.5% per year for women living outside of town.[8] Clearly the greatest need for family planning services was in rural areas, where 85% of Ethiopians lived.

The Mengistu government chose not to approve and implement the draft population policy written in 1988 specifically to address Ethiopia's high fertility rate. Despite devastating drought and famine conditions in the 1980s, fertility planning would not be a significant part of national policy at a time when every possible young male was being drafted and sent to the battlefront in Eritrea. Nevertheless a number of community-based pilot and demonstration projects were conducted in various parts of the country by non-governmental organizations such as the Family Guidance Association of Ethiopia, Pathfinder, and Save the Children (U.S). These efforts showed the feasibility of providing easily accessible family planning services and that a high percentage of fertile-age women had major unmet needs for contraception. Distribution of low-cost oral contraceptive pills by trained community residents was a practical option that also contributed to the financial support for ongoing services by "community health agents."[9] In the Gondar region, including the Kossoye area, the Family Guidance Association of Ethiopia began outreach services to rural populations in 1995.[10] Despite a slow but steady growth of contraceptive usage, the national average of contraceptive prevalence was only 8% in 2001.[11]

During this time population pressures in Kossoye increased dramatically. In the 1965 census, a total of 141 persons and 25 households were listed in Cherema and Zinjero Wuha. By the 1994 census that number had increased to 1008 persons and 192 households. Ten years later it was 1318 persons living in 290 households. A small part of this extraordinary growth was a result of the villagization campaign in 1986 and 1987 that transformed Cherema and Zinjero Wuha into Kossoye "town." But natural increase accounts for most of the population growth in the village as well as in the parish as a whole, which grew from an estimated 3,000 in 1967 to over 8,000 by 2007, despite a major out-migration of young people and deaths due to AIDS.[12]

Some Kossoyans understood that they had a land and population problem. In 1994 Kes Sisay said: "Every house has seven, eight, nine, ten children. What will be the future if they have children? They have no place outside of Kossoye."[13] His uncle Tagele focused on the difficulty of feeding so many people. "The old times were very, very good. Everything was cheap. We could invite a guest to have coffee or beer even for 10 or 15 cents. Now it costs 5 birr. Today there are many stomachs to be filled, many, many children."[14] A 29-year-old who had been married since the age of 17 but had only one child saw the problem starkly: "If it continues like this I will live worse than my parents and my children worse than me.

The main reason is population growth. Sometimes I have hope. But many times I cannot tell about the future or have hope....I do not know what to do."[15] Kes Eshete, who like Taye in 1967 failed to convince his wife to use an IUD, put the matter succinctly: "Population growth is happening. Land share is decreasing from time to time. I see life problems will be hard in the future."[16]

Land Shortage

Population growth directly impacted the quality of life in Kossoye since resources of arable land were fixed and most Kossoye families relied on agriculture for food and cash. While more families in the parish had access to land in 1994 than in the 1960s, the size of landholdings was less than half of what it had been. In 1994 the Development Agent from the Ministry of Agriculture reported that the 16 model farmers in the area worked plots ranging from ¼ hectare to 2 hectares. Herd sizes were also smaller because of disease and, more importantly, less grazing land. "A rich farmer might have 15 sheep, two cows, four oxen, one to two horses," said the Development Agent. An average farmer might have a total of five cows and sheep. Poor farmers had no cattle at all.[17]

These landholdings and livestock herds were obviously inadequate for supporting Kossoye's large households. Comparing conditions during his youth to those in old age, a 78-year-old farmer in the neighboring *kebele* put it this way: "It was better during my childhood. We had land. There were few people. The time was better. This time is dark."[18] Another old farmer in Cherema noted that "we were kings, we were rich" during the time of Haile Sellassie. "Now everything is going down. One reason is the increased number of people. Two, the land used to be bigger." Looking into the future, this farmer predicted problems for his children "because they will not have land. They will be thieves instead of farmers."[19]

The highland climate that allowed only one crop per year put even more pressure on the land. Plowing usually began in February, with poorer farmers borrowing oxen from wealthier neighbors. Limited availability of ox power meant that fields were plowed two rather than four times. Barley and wheat would be planted in June, weeded in July and August, and harvested between October and January. Farmers in the highlands of Ethiopia had followed this cycle for millennia.

In the 1990s everyone complained about reduced yields. Some blamed climate conditions and pests. Others noted soil exhaustion. "Today is the worst time of my life," said a farmer in his 70s, "because the land cannot give us as much as we want, like the old days. Every year it is decreasing. During the early years of my marriage, we had lots of cattle and crops. But land is getting infertile." He went on to note that land requires rest, but people now had so little land that they could not afford to allow fallow periods.[20]

Reduced land holdings encouraged a few people to plant vegetable gardens, but the Development Agent noted that "it is uncommon to plant vegetables." He had tried to teach people how to plant backyard gardens, with carrots, cabbage, peas, and peppers, as had a teacher in the local school.[21] "But for reasons we cannot identify they did not grow well. There is something that dried up the garden. We gave that up and started to teach them theoretically—types of erosion, the types of garden they could have, crop rotation, types of farming."[22]

One reason for the poor success of vegetable gardens may be that in the 1990s, eucalyptus nurseries, one of Taye and Ferrede's innovations from the 1960s, occupied lands appropriate for gardens. The Development Agent estimated that families earned 500 to 4,000 EB a year from tree farming (about $60 to $500 U.S.) and said that many families "might not have survived without eucalyptus trees."[23] The need for cash also caused people to plant trees instead of vegetables in locations near wells, where there is water run-off, or along stream beds.

People talked about choosing clothes over food: "In the old times, there was lots of milk and butter," said Taye's younger brother Tagele, then 76 years old. "No one was hungry. But at that time there were few clothes and no sanitation. Homes were not as clean. That is the only bad thing. Now we can have good clothing but not enough food. Children today have good clothes but they are hungry. And their houses are clean."[24] A 42-year-old military veteran emphasized the greater market and educational opportunities: "There was quantity of food in the past. Now people distribute their wealth for clothes, for educating their children."[25]

Nutrition

Population increase and land shortage obviously had negative effects on nutrition. Although little applied nutritional research was conducted during the *Derg* regime, in 1991 Zein reported an 11% prevalence of low birthweight infants born in health centers and hospitals in the Gondar region, reflecting significant chronic malnutrition of pregnant women.[26] Students and staff who were part of the Ethiopia-McGill Public Health Training Program in the late 1980s and early 1990s did epidemiological studies on nutrition problems in several communities in the south and west of Ethiopia that revealed widespread chronic malnutrition.[27] Catastrophic drought and famine from 1983 to 1987 caused a number of international organizations to collaborate with the Ethiopian government in establishing "famine early warning systems" (FEWS) to assist in relief and rehabilitation. Nutritional surveys using height and weight measurements were conducted as part of food distribution programs by government and non-government organizations such as CARE and Save the Children.[28]

Applied nutritional research increased in many areas following the end of the *Derg* regime. Severe vitamin A deficiencies were found in Hararghe, with nearly 15% of children having "Bitot Spots" and 19% experiencing night blindness.[29] A study in the mid-1990s showed that 18% of children born in the Gondar Hospital and surrounding health centers were found to have low birth-weights, indicating widespread malnutrition of women of childbearing age.[30]

Relationships between the education of girls and the nutrition of their infants and young children were examined in two regions of Ethiopia. A 1996 study in the Guraghe zone showed that 52% of children who had illiterate mothers suffered stunting, but when mothers had been to school, only 22% were stunted. For each year of a girl's education they calculated an 8% reduction in child mortality.[31] Another landmark study conducted in 2001 in Hadiya in southern Ethiopia compared mothers from the lowlands with their counterparts in the highlands. Even though households at lower altitudes had more land to cultivate and owned more animals, girls and women had less education, and 31% of their children were stunted. Mothers in the higher altitudes were generally better educated and 19% of their children suffered chronic protein-energy malnutrition. Stunting due to chronic under-nutrition was particularly noted.[32] The North Gondar zone reportedly had 66% stunting of children in 1992, and the Amhara region as a whole a prevalence of 60% stunting in 1998. Nutritional deficiencies of vitamin A, iodine, and iron were also increasing, according to this study. A review of the status and trends of malnutrition in Ethiopia published in 2001 concluded that several kinds of malnutrition are steadily increasing. In 2005 when *The Epidemiology and Ecology of Health and Disease in Ethiopia* was published, the authors wrote that the "prevalence of stunting in Ethiopia is among the highest in the world and is shown to be increasing."[33] A comprehensive survey of the literature cited low agricultural production, low food consumption, and high rates of diseases as important causes.[34] Decreasing land availability per capita, falling agricultural productivity of cultivated soil, and diminishing per capita income were also cited. Delay in adding supplementary foods to breast feeding, low frequency of infant and child feeding, and untreated diarrhea and respiratory infections contributed significantly to undernourishment of infants and children.

The present authors conducted a health survey in collaboration with the University of Gondar in early 2005 using approximately the same methods employed by students in their research projects in Kossoye during the 1960s. In 1965 it had been possible to examine nearly all the population of Cherema and Zinjero Wuha. By 2005 the population had increased so much that a systematic random sampling was used to select and examine members of 192 households. The Kemant populations in the Cherema and Zinjero Wuha neighborhoods of Kossoye were compared with those living there in 1967 and with the Amhara population now living on the opposite side of the highway in the neighborhood called Gedeye.

The results of the nutritional analyses are striking. In 1967 16.7% of Kemant girls under 15 had stunting. By 2005, thirty-eight years later, the rate had increased to 26.5%. During this same period malnutrition in women over 15 increased from 15.4% to 34.6% and Kemant women had a slightly higher rate of malnutrition than men. In 2005 Amhara girls under 15 were stunted at a rate of 46.5%, while women over 15 years had 30% (Figure 1).

Stunting among Kemant boys rose even more dramatically. In 1967 it was 20%. By 2005 it reached 42.4%. In 2005 half (50%) of Amhara boys were stunted. The only group that showed no significant change were Kemant males over 15, where stunting was 27.3% in 1967 and 28% in 2005. In 2005 Amhara males over 15 in the Gedeye neighborhood had a rate of 28.8%, almost the same as their Kemant neighbors across the highway (Figure 2).

Figure 7.1: Proportion of Stunted Female Population by Year, Age and Ethnicity; Kossoye, Ethiopia

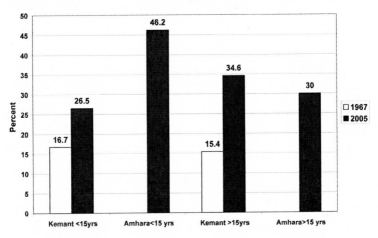

Figure 7.2: Proportion of Stunted Male Population by Year, Age and Ethnicity; Kossoye, Ethiopia

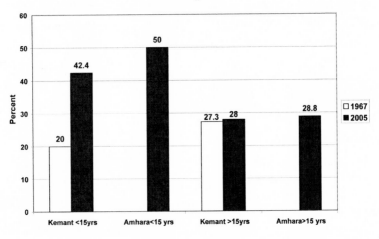

Figure 7.3: Proportion of Stunted Population by Year, Age and Ethnicity; Kossoye, Ethiopia

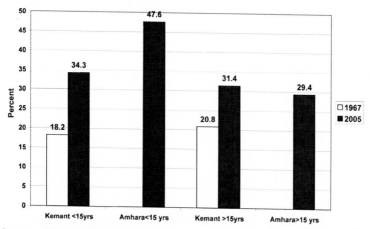

Sources (Figs 1-3): Based upon census and health surveys conducted by faculty and staff at the University of Gonder.

This analysis indicates that in the past four decades nutritional status has seriously deteriorated among Kemant women and children (male and female). It also demonstrates that in 2005 an alarming 48% of Amhara children under 15 years of age were suffering from severe chronic malnutrition. That both boys and men in the Kemant community were more malnourished than females in 1967 is unexpected. Perhaps females of all ages had less malnutrition than males because of their access to food during preparation of meals. Differences in stunting between Amhara and Kemant children in 2005 are also dramatic. One factor may be that locally a higher percentage of Kemant parents have some schooling. Another factor (cited by the local people) may be that Kemant families share food more equitably than Amhara families. The lingering effects of villagization may explain some of the greater poverty of newcomers to Kossoye.

Health

During the *Derg* era most health services in Kossoye were curtailed, because the highway from Gondar to the north was closed to nearly all traffic.[35] In the late 1980s one resident who had worked previously as a traditional health practitioner underwent training as a "Community Health Agent" in a large-scale training program with over 20,000 participants. He was supposed to provide basic health services in the Kossoye area, but without supervisory or logistical support, he returned to his practice of traditional medicine, adding "injections" to his herbal treatments.[36] The Dabat Training Health Center was severely damaged during battles between insurgents and government forces in the late 1980s and in 1991. Though some health posts were built and staffed in other parts of Ethiopia during the *Derg* period, none was constructed in Kossoye.[37]

The war complicated outreach to some rural communities. Fear of violence and hostility from local community residents toward government workers was a genuine concern. So too was a lack of trained health workers, a result of the *Derg's* decision to emphasize the training of clinical physicians and nurses instead of health officers and community health nurses. As noted earlier, in 1978 the Public Health College and Training Center was radically reorganized and renamed the Gondar College of Medical Sciences (GCMS). Strategic goals were changed by the *Derg* government to focus on hospital and clinic-based diagnosis and treatment of patients, rather than on health center and community-based approaches which emphasize disease prevention, health promotion, and treatment of common diseases. Immunization programs in rural communities continued. But medical doctors and clinical nurses were posted primarily in hospitals and clinics. For residents of Kossoye this meant that access to modern health care was practically nonexistent unless they traveled to the clinic in Ambaghiorgis or the Gondar hospital.

Services improved in 1991 after the new EPRDF government came to power. The government repaired the Dabat Health Center and the Debarek community offered the old *kebele* offices to serve as a new Training Health Center for the College. Medical and nursing students from the Gondar College of Medical Sciences began to receive some practical training in market towns of the highlands north of Gondar. With the assistance of the British Red Cross, the spring at Cherema and Zinjero Wuha was rebuilt with an extensive gravity water flow system. A fence was built to protect the distribution site, and a daytime guard was promised compensation by community members. The community did not meet its responsibilities to provide payment to the guard, however, and within a few months she left her assignment.

In 1995 the Federal Democratic Republic of Ethiopia reversed *Derg* policies and launched a new health services program of primary care focusing on a rapid increase in the number of health centers in market towns and health posts in surrounding rural communities. The training of health officers was reinstituted in 1996 as post-basic training for experienced nurses to become health officers in Gondar and Jimma. In addition, two new health sciences faculties were established at Haramaya University near Harar in southeastern Ethiopia and Dilla in the south.

Further investment in health services for the inadequately served rural populations began in 2002 when the government launched a massive effort to train 25,000 women with secondary school credentials to staff the Health Services Extension Program. These community-based Health Services Extension Workers are expected to live and work in under-served communities such as Kossoye, supervised by district (*woreda*) health offices and local health centers. In 2004 the government initiated a large "Accelerated Health Officer Training Program" to prepare 5,000 health officers for work in 3,000 health centers by 2010, mostly in newly constructed or renovated buildings.

The government built a handsome four-room health post in Kossoye in 1998, but nurses and support personnel were not assigned until 2004. Basic services were offered after that, and the building was also used for outreach immunization programs from Ambaghiorgis. Monthly family planning services were provided from the branch office of the Family Guidance Association of Ethiopia program in Gondar. In 2006 two young women trained as Health Services Extension Workers were assigned to work in the neighboring communities around Cherema, Zinjero Wuha, and Gedeye. They do vaccinations, promote family planning, treat uncomplicated illnesses, and engage in health education. Kossoye was also chosen in 2006 as one of the first communities to receive semiannual Vitamin A and de-worming medicine for children under five years of age.

Despite these improvements, in January 2005 the authors were struck by the large number of people who requested medical help during a period of remapping, census-taking, and interviewing. In collaboration with the University of Gondar they carried out a health survey using several indicators employed by students in the 1960s (as described earlier). The survey was completed in March 2005, with special attention given to eye infections (especially trachoma), skin lesions, intestinal parasites, and nutritional status. Nearly all the members of 192 households in Cherema and Zinjero Wuha were examined in the course of five intensive days at the health post. The results were illuminating, particularly when compared with those from 1965.

Table 7.1 Health Indicators, 1965 and 2005

Disease	1965	2005
Skin infections and lesions	84%	5%
Intestinal Parasites	79%	28%
Eye Infections/Trachoma	77%	93%

Sources: Reports on community health status, conducted by the University of Gondar and its predecessors, 1965 and 2005 (Private Archives).

The table shows that significant progress has been achieved in reducing the rates of both skin infections and intestinal parasites. The reduction of intestinal parasites from 79% to 28% is striking. That scabies and other skin lesions fell from 84% to 5% was unexpected. The increase in the prevalence of eye infections (primarily trachoma, from 77% to 93%) was sobering.[38]

The dramatic decline in the incidence of skin lesions and intestinal parasites likely was influenced by the weekly hygiene examinations of all students at the school, as well as by the installation of protected water sources. The higher prevalence of eye infections may be explained in part by the greater awareness and competence of clinicians to recognize trachoma now, as compared with forty years ago. The high prevalence also shows that personal and household hygiene continues to be a major problem. Contributing factors include a lack of latrines, animals living close to families, large populations of flies (especially Musca sorbens, a face and fluid-seeking species of the domestic housefly),[39] and neglect of facial hygiene.

Reliable epidemiological data on HIV/AIDS cases are difficult to obtain. During the health survey in 2005, at least two young people who were carried to the health post to be examined appeared to have clinical symptoms of advanced AIDS. A husband and wife who taught in the Kossoye school died in 2005, probably with AIDS. A knowledgeable woman from Kossoye who now works in Gondar said that nearly every family had lost at least one member to the "dread disease."[40] Voluntary counseling, testing, and free anti-retro-viral therapy are now available at the University Hospital in Gondar. Recent government policy has been established that diagnostic and treatment capacities for HIV/AIDs will be extended to health centers in the near future.

Family Planning

In March 2005, Dennis Carlson visited Shashitu in her home. Then 80 years old, she was stooped and suffered from respiratory problems. Her husband had passed away several years before. One of her daughters lived with her. Carlson asked whether she remembered the conversation about family planning forty years ago. "Oh yes!" she replied, "You gave me back my health. If I hadn't started family planning then, I don't know what would have happened. My neighbors too were very grateful."

The story of Shashitu's acceptance of family planning in 1967 was encouraging but it did not forecast future choices. During the *Derg* regime government health centers and hospital clinics offered limited family planning services, and a number of community-based distribution projects were established by NGOs.[41] But the government resisted launching large-scale family planning services for rural communities.

In 1993 the new TPLF/EPRDF government promulgated an official population policy which emphasized the essential need for providing family planning services. The government and NGOs expanded efforts in their clinical facilities, located in towns and in community-based programs. The Family Guidance Association of Ethiopia expanded its outreach services in the North Gondar zone including Kossoye. Community Based Reproductive Health

Workers were trained who went from house to house selling oral contraceptives and condoms at subsidized prices, gaining small incomes. Their roles also included educating men and women on the desirability of using family planning services. Though intrauterine contraceptive devices are safe, effective, and much less expensive, injectables (such as Depo-Provera) have the attraction of being given by needle, a method often preferred by rural Ethiopians.

In 1994, the German international technical assistance agency (GTZ) funded a major study of knowledge, attitudes, and practices in family planning in North Gondar, including Kossoye. Dr. Shabbir Ismael made a report that focused on 201 fertile-aged women living in two of the Kossoye neighborhoods.[42] Remarkable changes had taken place since the 1960s. Eighty-nine (89) percent said they approved of spacing their own pregnancies; 80% approved of family spacing methods and thought it necessary to take measures against rapid family expansion; 70% wanted more information about family planning; 59% said their husbands or companions supported child spacing; 56% believed that having many children was harmful. The average number of children desired was six.[43] In previous decades the responses might have been "as many as possible" or "ten or twelve."

Women were also more ready to use contraceptives than they had been in 1967, when Shashitu asked for the IUD. In a survey conducted in 1998 with 201 local women, 136 individuals reported that they had heard about family planning; and 160 responded affirmatively to the statement that "it is necessary to take measures against rapid family expansion." Fertile women in the Kossoye area responded favorably when outreach services began in their community. Different methods were available: oral contraceptives, Depo-Provera, Norplant, and condoms, though not intra-uterine devices. Services included post-abortion aspiration of incomplete abortions, a need which may have been increased by interruptions in the supply system, forcing some women to miss two or three treatments.

By 2005 between 250 and 300 women in the *kebele* were using family planning methods of various kinds. These women were nearly all from the Kossoye area, with a total estimated 6,000 residents. Thus the contraceptive prevalence rate may be estimated to be in the range of 20 to 25%, quite remarkable given the national rate thought to be less than 10%.

It is noteworthy that use of family planning is highest in the Zinjero Wuha and Cherema hamlets.[44] These are the original Kossoye neighborhoods which have had more than forty years of community discussions about family planning, as well as relatively easy access to elementary education. These are also the neighborhoods with the highest population density, suggesting that attitudes and behaviors associated with town life in Ethiopia are making their way into Kossoye.

It is also noteworthy that some members of the local Ethiopian Orthodox Church community have changed their minds about family planning. After years of discussing the topic and insisting that birth is a blessing from God, Kes Sisay is persuaded that there is a religious precedent for family planning: the proscription of sex during fasting and other religious holidays. He also provided a pragmatic explanation for the new Biblical interpretation: "The economy is going downwards. An average family of 12 now has only one *tind* of land (1/4 hectare), so people can't produce enough food."[45] Another priest, Kes Eshete Bogale, strongly favored family planning in 1967, but later changed his mind, possibly because of his wife's unwillingness to accept an IUD after delivery of her eighth baby. In an interview in 1998 he said he truly understood the value of family planning. He could see the population problem.[46]

Positions on family planning will change according to circumstances if not policy. In January of 2005, in the presence of his large extended family, Kes Eshete, then 85 years old, reflected on his nine surviving children: "One is in Israel, has his own car and garage. Two daughters are housewives, 3 sons are farmers, and the others work for the Ministry of Education." Then he went on to say: "If we had had family planning, we would not have had the last four who are the most successful. All my children learned how to read and write. The early kids are less literate. The last three kids finished grade 12."[47] Three of his first eight died in childhood.

Positions on family planning are most clearly stated among the educated youngsters. In 2005 focus group interviews conducted by Dr. Daniel Shibru among the eighth-grade boys and girls at the Kossoye school, the students saw themselves pursuing more education and work somewhere else. Although they came from families with five or six children, most went on to say that they themselves wanted only one or two children; the highest number of children desired was four. The children also discussed career aspirations: nurse, teacher, government minister, journalist, judge, lawyer, archeologist, AIDs researcher, agricultural planner, and agronomist. Their understanding of their own wellbeing rested on what they could secure for themselves in salaried positions.[48]

These eighth graders in the Kossoye School are some of the most modern members of the community. Probably their families are also more modern than their neighbors—explaining why they have five or six rather than nine or ten children. These children have benefited from a school curriculum that includes some sex education and family planning. They are aware of the problems in the agricultural economy; in fact, they are the ones that their families have designated to go to school rather than farm. Not one boy or girl aspired to a traditional occupation. Other children their age who are not in school may not have the same clear rationalizations for limiting family size and pursuing education. But virtually all children in Kossoye understand that they live in a world with many people and little land; most understand that the new reality of life in Ethiopia includes limiting family size.

Conclusion

In the 1950s social scientists expressed concern about what difficulties rapid population growth would cause rural societies as they tried to modernize.[49] In the 1960s, Dennis Carlson discussed family planning with women in Cherema and Zinjero Wuha, and five individuals chose to have IUDs. There were also debates at the Haile Sellassie I University (discussed in chapter one) about whether Ethiopia needed a population program. At that time, however, most people in Ethiopia were convinced that procreation was an unlimited blessing.

Since the 1980s, rapid population growth has been understood in Ethiopia's modern sector to be a major impediment to development. It has become clear that all human societies, perhaps especially those in Africa, have limits to how many people they can support. Given the terrible famines of the last thirty years in Ethiopia, two of which contributed to the downfall of central governments, it is surprising that positive policy positions took so long to be developed and implemented. In 2005 the United Nations agencies predicted the population of Ethiopia might double over the next 30 years from 77 million to more than 150 million.

In Kossoye serious behavioral and attitudinal changes are taking place. In the 1960s, a few women in Kossoye led the way in asking for family planning. Forty years later, as shrinking landholdings have resulted in increased malnutrition, more people in the area understand the need to limit family size. The current EPRDF government has commendable goals for reducing the rapid population growth rates. In March 2007 the Ministry of Finance and Economic Development endorsed a draft document which establishes population councils in all regions. The purposes of these councils will be "coordinating and leading population issues incorporated under the five-year development Strategy."[50] Work remains on implementation.

Notes

1. On this topic of change in rural Ethiopia in the 1990s, see Wendy James, Donald Donham, Eisei Kurimoto, Alessandro Triulzi, eds., *Remapping Ethiopia: Socialism and After* (Oxford: James Currey, 2002); James C. McCann, *People of the Plow: An Agricultural History of Ethiopia, 1800-1990* (Madison: University of Wisconsin Press, 1995); Abebe Zegeye and Sigfried Pausewang, eds, *Ethiopia in Change: Peasantry, Nationalism and Democracy* (British Academic Pres, 1994); and Bahru Zewde and Siegfried Pausewang, eds., *Ethiopia: The Challenge of Democracy from Below* (Uppsala: Nordiska Afrikainstituet; Addis Ababa: Forum for Social Studies, 2002).

2. Declaration of Alma Ata, 1978.

3. Assefa Hailemariam and Helmut Kloos, "Population," in *The Ecology of Health and Disease in Ethiopia,* Helmut Kloos and Zein Ahmed Zein, eds., (Westview Press, 1993), 58.

4. Mehari Wolde Ab, "Demography and Health Planning," in *The Ecology of Health and Disease in Ethiopia* ed. by Zein Ahmed Zein and Helmut Kloos (Addis Ababa: Ministry of Health, 1988), 43.

5. Mehari Wolde Ab, "Demosgraphy and Health Planning," 43.

6. Mengistu Asnake and Charles Larson, "Focus Group Identification of Barriers to the Use of Modern Contraception in the Gara Muleta District of East Hararghe," *Ethiopian Journal of Health Development*, 1991, Vol. 5:1, 29-34.

7. Assefa Hailemariam and Helmut Kloos, "Population," 58.

8. Desta Shamebo, "Epidemiology for public health research and action in a developing society: The Butajira Rural Health Project," *Ethiopian Journal of Health Development*, 1994, Vol. 8:1, 22-23.

9. Dennis G. Carlson, Seifu Wolde Abraham, and Mesganaw Tamene, "A Two Year Progress Report on an integrated pilot community based family planning project in Efratana Timuga Awraja in Northern Shewa." Paper presented at the Second Annual Scientific conference of the Ethiopian Public Health Association, Addis Ababa, August 22-24, 1991.

10. Interview at Gondar Branch of Family Guidance Association of Ethiopia, Feb. 2006.

11. Yohannes Fitaw, Yemane Berhane, Alemayehu Worku, "Differentials of fertility in rural Butajira," *Ethiopian Journal of Health Development*, April 2003, Vol. 17:1, 17-26.

12. Interview 92, May 14, 2006.

13. Interview 28, February 21, 1994.

14. Interview 21, February 18, 1994.

15. Interview 26, February 17, 1994.

16. Interview 52, April 29, 1998.

17. Interview 8, February 20, 1994.

18. Interview 11, February 1994.

19. Interview 12, February 1994.

20. Interview 22, February 1994.

21. Interview 8, February 20, 1994.

22. Interview 13, February 17, 1994.

23. Interview 8, February 20, 1994.

24. Interview 21, February 18, 1994.

25. Interview 19, February 17, 1994.

26. Zein Ahmed Zein and Alemayehu Worku, "The distribution of low birth weight in the Gondar Administrative Region, Northwestern Ethiopia," *Ethiopian Journal of Health Development*, 1991, Vol. 5:2, 71-74.

27. Louise Pilote, George Olwit, Gebreselassie Okubagzi, Charles Larson, "Community based nutritional study: Geruke Jimate Peasants Association, Illubabor Region, Ethiopia," *Ethiopian Journal of Health Development*, 1991, Vol. 5:1, 25-28.

28. Judith Appleton, ed., "Drought Relief in Ethiopia: Planning and Management of Feeding Programmes," 1987, Save the Children (UK), London.

29. Jemal Haidar and Hana Neka Tibeb, "Xerophthalmia in children of Torbayo, West Hararghe," *Ethiopian Journal of Health Development*, 1998, Vol. 12:1, 39-43.

30. Melkie Edris and Getnet Erakil, "The prevalence of low birth weight delivery in Gondar Region, Northwest Ethiopia," *Ethiopian Journal of Health Development*, 1996, Vol. 10:3, 149-152.

31. Timotewos Genebo, Woldemariam Girma, Jamal Haider, and Tsegaye Demsse, "The association of children's nutritional status to maternal education in Zigbaboto, Guragie Zone, Ethiopia," *Ethiopian Journal of Health Development*, 1999, Vol.13:1, 55-62.

32. Tsegaye Demissie, Yared Mekonen and Jemal Haider, *Ethiopian Journal of Health Development*, 2003, Vol. 17:3, 189-196.

33. Jemal Haidar, Damen Haile Mariam, Tsegaye Demisse and Helmut Kloos, "Food, Diet and Nutrition" in Yemane Berhane, Damen Haile Mariam, Helmut Kloos, eds, *The Epidemiology and Ecology of Health and Disease in Ethiopia* (Addis Ababa: Shama Books, 2005): 95-97.

34. Zawditu Getahun, Kalbessa Urga, Timotewos Genebo, Ayele Nigatu, "Review of the status of malnutrition and trends in Ethiopia," *Ethiopian Journal of Health Development*, 2001, Vol. 15:2, 55-74.

35. Interview 6, February 16, 1994.

36. Interview 6, February 16, 1994.

37. Health Posts are intended to serve as the base of operations for Health Services Extension Agents (HSEWS). These workers are

supposed to give nearly all efforts to prevention of diseases and promotion of health.

38. It was not possible to use precisely the same methods and criteria that students used in 1965-7 since the descriptions of methods were incomplete in available copies of their work. The overwhelming prevalence of trachoma in present day Ethiopia is much better understood than it was in the 1960s. It is possible that the prevalence is roughly the same now. We do not know whether the prevalence of intestinal parasites was based on examination of specimens in saline solutions which were centrifuged or not. In 2005 the feces samples in saline solutions were examined microscopically at the Kossoye health post without centrifuging.

39. The Musca sorbens subspecies of houseflies breed in fresh human and animal feces and is attracted almost entirely to facial fluids, particularly around the eyes of children.

40. Interview 7, January 6, 2005.

41. Community-based projects were introduced in the late 1980s by NGOs such as Save the Children (US) which were also effective in providing small but significant income for Community Health Agents who sold contraceptive pills for 25 to 50 cents.

42. Shabir Ismael, "Family Planning Survey in Gondar, April 1994," unpublished, financed by GTZ (Germany).

43. Total number of women interviewed was 1619, of which 201 women were from Kossoye Bata and Kossoye Medhane Alem.

44. Interview 21, January 2005.

45. Interview 70, January 5, 2005.

46. Interview 52, April 29, 1998.

47. Interview 64, January 5, 2005.

48. Interviews 5 and 6, January 5, 2005.

49. See for example Gunnar Myrdal, *Economic Theory and Underdeveloped Regions* (London: University Paperbacks, 1963, first published

1957) and Carlo M. Cipolla, *The Economic History of World Population* (Middlesex, England: Penguin Books, 1962).

50. "Ministry endorses draft document establishing population councils," *The Ethiopian Herald*, 2007, Vol. 63:131, 1.

1995: Protected spring fenced to keep animals away.

2005: Threshing grain in the village.

1998: Kes Eshete Bogale at the Medhane Alem
tree nursery, which operates under the auspices
of the Ministry of Agriculture.

2005: A roadside eucalyptus market,
where trucks load poles and firewood for
transportation to area towns.

2005: The eucalyptus forest (approximately 20 hectares) owned by the Medhane Alem Church.

2005: Farmers weighing grain in front of the town center, which includes three offices for local officials, a solar cell phone, a storage facility, and a failed tool manufacturing facility.

CHAPTER EIGHT

A MODERN TOWN

❖ ❖ ❖

In 2007, the beginning of the third millennium in the Ethiopian calendar, many Kossoyans felt they were close to achieving goals articulated by Taye, his father, and cousins when they first settled in the area in 1945. Late in 2006 a police station was built and two policemen hired. The Kossoye station is connected by solar-powered phone to the district station, 8 kilometers away by well maintained road in Ambagiorghis. In the summer of 2007 Kossoye was connected to the national electric grid, thus opening the way for three shops with televisions and a bar with draft beer. In early December a Kossoyan who had made a fortune importing goods from China arranged to buy land from the school for a new hotel, at the edge of the escarpment where Haile Sellassie had entertained Queen Elizabeth II in 1965. Preparations were also underway for a new market located on the broad field between the school and the health post.

These long-anticipated developments have not been without controversy. Modern Kossoyans, the people who have been to school and who now need to have occupations beyond those found in the local agricultural economy, hope for employment from expanded government services (schools, security, health, administrators) and commerce (small family businesses). The traditionalists are worried about town life. They do not want prices to increase, robbers to take their goods, or family members to risk their subsistence by spending money on consumer goods.

Continuity has been noted as a theme in Ethiopian society through the tumult of the twentieth century.[1] In Kossoye, continuity is evident. The Ethiopian Orthodox Church remains the most powerful local institution. Most of the leading community members continue to support large families through agriculture and supplementary cash crops.

But change is a more important theme. Cherema and Zinjero Wuha are now at the center of a growing town with many more people living in contiguous neighborhoods. (See Map 5.) The school, built in collaboration with the Swedish International Development Agency, educates over 1200 students. A town government organizes local activities: a mill, storage facilities, a small factory for agricultural equipment (currently not in use), a health post, a militia, and a judicial council. Taye's daughter owns and operates a new private diesel-powered mill that draws farmers from the lowlands. Cars and busses pick up and drop off passengers and goods from destinations near and far. Trucks load up stacks of eucalyptus trees, now the most significant cash crop, for a thriving urban construction market. Most of the twenty plus teachers in the local school commute daily from Gondar, providing an infusion of modern ideas and cash. Many Kossoyans have traveled to Gondar, Addis Ababa, and Sudan.

These changes reflect the pull of globalization processes found in rural communities all over the world.[2] In Kossoye, the changes reveal a generational divide between the traditionalists and the moderns. Of course this is a complex divide. But one historical marker is the Revolution. The pre-revolutionary generation still farm land that they inherited from their parents, grow most of their own crops, dress in traditional clothes, live with spouses chosen by their parents, worship at the Orthodox Church, and learn the news at the Sunday parish meeting (*senbete*).

Map 5: Kossoye Town in 2005

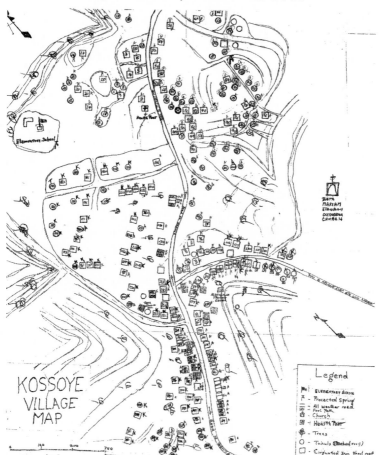

Source: This map was prepared by students in the Environmental Health
Program at the University of Gondar in January 2005.

The post-revolutionary children and grandchildren have
lives that are more modern.[3] As children they go to school.
As young adults they look for non-agricultural work, because
they do not inherit land, and landholdings have become so
small they cannot be effectively divided any further. They
choose their own spouses. They buy their own food and so
need cash for the market or local store. They wear modern

imports from China, Europe, and the United States. They get their news from radios, which they are keen to own. They continue to go to the Orthodox Christian church at home, but when they travel to the city, some attend Pentecostal and other Protestant services.[4]

Occupations

For at least twenty years Kossoyans have experienced a transitional economy based in agriculture but with increasing occupational diversity. In the 1965 census taken by students from the Haile Sellassie I Public Health College, there were only 4 job categories for the 141 individuals in Cherema and Zinjero Wuha: farmers (23%), housewives (20%), maids (12%), and shepherds (12%). By 1994 there were at least 10 occupational categories plus categories for the retired and unemployed. (See Table 8.1.)

For about thirty years, from 1965 to 1994, the percentage of men in traditional occupations remained quite stable, presumably similar to what it had been in the nineteenth century and before. In the thirty years since 1965 their proportion to the rest of the population remained steady at about 23% (though the numbers of farmers increased from 32 to 231). The number and percentage of shepherds increased, from 6% (9) to 11.6% (117).

By the time of the 2004 census, however, the reliance on agriculture as an occupation had declined. The number of farmers had increased from 231 to 250, but this was a significant decline in the percentage of the whole, from 22.9 to 18.3% of all Kossoyans. The statistics on changes in the shepherd population are unavailable because of a census-taking error in 2004. It is likely, however, that there were more shepherds than the 117 noted in 1994 (11.6%), though a smaller share of the whole.

Table 8.1 Occupations in Kossoye, 1965, 1994, 2004

Occupations	1965		1994		2004	
Farmer	32	22.7%	231	24.5%	250	19.0%
Trader	0	0.0%	3	0.3%	10	0.8%
Gov't. Worker	0	0.0%	5	0.5%	25	1.9%
Student	3	2.1%	108	11.5%	458	34.7%
Daily Laborer	0	0.0%	1	0.1%	47	3.6%
House-Wife	28	19.9%	148	15.7%	185	14.0%
House Worker/Maid	17	12.1%	41	4.4%	17	1.3%
Tella Seller	0	0.0%	6	0.6%	19	1.4%
Prostitute	0	0.0%	8	0.9%	3	0.2%
Shepherd	9	6.4%	117	12.4%	0	0.0%
Retired	0	0.0%	1	0.1%	1	0.1%
Unemployed	0	0.0%	17	1.8%	59	4.5%
Over 65 Yrs	5	3.5%	11	1.2%	11	0.8%
Under 7 Yrs	49	33.3%	244	25.9%	233	17.7%
Totals:	143	100.0%	941	100.0%	1318	100.0%

Sources: These statistics are compiled from the public health census reports collected by the College in 1965, 1994, and 2004.

The changes in traditional women's occupations have been more dramatic. Between 1965 and 1994 the percentage of housewives declined, from 20% (28) to 14.7% (148), and the percentage of maids dropped from 12% (17) to 4.1% (41). By 2004 only 13.6% of the females were housewives (n=185). The decline in the number and percentage of maids was more significant: from 4.1% in 1994 (n=41) to 1.2% in 2004 (n=17).

In the course of interviews none of the local people mentioned dramatic changes in traditional female roles. People were, however, concerned about inheritance. Before the nationalization of land in 1975 both men and women inherited real property as part of their dowries, assuming that their families had land to pass on to their children. There were fewer people then, and at least some families had several parcels of land that they could distribute among their children, females and males. As will be recalled, if women divorced, especially early in a marriage, they usually kept their own wealth. Their husbands would inherit their dowry land only if their wives died after some years of marriage.[5]

Since the socialist revolution dowries have included money and cattle but not land, because land no longer is legally transferable or inheritable. Rights to the land are usufruct (meaning that crops produced on the land belong to the farmer, though the land officially belongs to the state). One or two sons in a family may continue to live with the parents, taking care of them but also establishing user rights which the local government (*kebele*) often recognizes. Young women usually do not have this fall-back position. They are expected to marry or go to town, without specific rights or even a proxy claim to land.

A 65-year-old farmer explained his own strategy of land distribution for his 9 children (with two wives). Of the 6 children still living at home, he relied on two sons to farm the land. He assumed that the land would be divided between these two sons. "I don't know what the girls will do," he went on to say. It would seem he assumed that his land would be too small to offer to any of his daughters and their families.[6]

Another farmer in Ambaras had a similar strategy. Then 78 years old, he had 2 sons and 6 daughters. The older daughters had left home. The sons farmed their father's land and were beginning their own families. The 31-year-old was married and had two children. This son noted that he would like to have 3 sons and 3 daughters. When asked if all could be farmers, he said: "No, there won't be enough land, but I expect one to farm and two to go to school. I believe they will find work in the modern world as a mechanic, house builder, or something."[7] The three children he mentioned seem to be the boys. The girls, apparently, would simply find their own way.

The decline in traditional occupations has been offset by occupational development and education. For example, while in 1994 only 1.9% of the population (N=18 persons) was engaged in non-farming occupations, by 2004 that number had increased to 6% (n=79). The most dramatic increase was in the number of laborers, from 1 to 47. In the construction business in the Gondar region, day laborers can now be female as well as male, so it is reasonable to think that some laborers in Kossoye are women.

More women have also become teachers and students. In 1965, the school's first year, there were a total of 74 students in Kossoye, 66% of them female. During the Derg, student population increased slowly, less than 1 percent annually, so by 1994 the total number of students was only 162 (77% female). The next ten years saw dramatic increases in the student and teacher populations. By 2004 the number of students living in Kossoye was 458, a 33.6 percent increase of the total 1318. In the school enrollment figures for 2005, 59% were female. The number of teachers increased from .5 percent (5) of the whole population in 1994 to 1.8 percent (25) in 2004, in step with the increases in the student population. As shown in Table 8.2, school enrollment expanded about 7% per year from 1994 to 2005: from 162 to 1048.

Table 8.2 Summary of School Enrollments, 1965-2005

Year	Total	% Female	% Male
1965	74	66%	34%
1967	117	50%	50%
1994	162	77%	23%
1996	306	75%	25%
1998	501	64%	36%
2000	729	66%	34%
2005	1048	59%	41%

Sources: These enrollment numbers have been collected by the authors from the school directors since 1965. Students are from many communities in addition to those in the Kossoye parish.

The increased school enrollment is due partly to an appreciation for the value of learning, but it is also born out of necessity. There are no longer any parents in the Kossoye area who have several plots of land that can be parceled out to their children. At best, farming is an occupation for only one or two children, the ones parents designate as their own social security plan. These children will have a place to live with their parents, and probably their parents' land, but they will also take care of mother and father in their old age. The other children go to school. Some boys and girls as young as eight walk more than 20 kilometers to school, up to the highlands on Sundays and back to the lowlands on Friday afternoons. About ten women have moved from the lowlands so their children can attend the Kossoye school. The *kebele* chairman explained in 2005 why all his children go to school: "There is a shortage of land. If kids do not go to school, they get married at 16 and live at home. We prefer they become educated and move elsewhere. All my nine children (and one orphan) go to school. They work in shifts for cattle. Everybody goes to school, because of land shortage."[8]

In Kossoye girls are the ones who most clearly do not have a place in the local economy and thus are in school. Since 1965 about two-thirds of all students in the Kossoye school have been girls. The low point for male attendance, 23%, was 1991, the last year of the Derg. Parents desired to protect their sons from military service, and schools served as major military impressment stations. The high point for male attendance, 50%, was 1967. A female school director in Kossoye commented that in two other schools in the highlands where she had worked she observed a similar preponderance of female students.

Considering the subordinate position of women in most of Ethiopian society, this is paradoxical. After all, if boys are favored, why are there more girls in school? One director of the Kossoye school reported that he had argued with parents that boys also needed education, but said the parents "don't listen. They say…who can help me [when I become old]? Therefore I will never send a boy but you can take a girl."[9]

Tagele explained the preference for boys this way: "It is because of the family work. As long as the family relies on farming, whenever he has sons he will allot them to the different chores: looking after the cattle, the sheep, gathering food for the animals, plowing the fields. But if he has daughters, it is only the mother who must be helped. So if there are more than one, they will be sent to school."[10]

Deciding to send girls to school is thus a pragmatic calculation of household usefulness rather than a belief about individual talent or the utility of education. In the presence of his wife and daughter, an old farmer was asked if women do better in school than men. He responded: "Boys are better than girls [in school]. Here in our rural area, we see the boys pass and the girls fail." When the question was turned to his wife and daughter who were sitting in the room listening in, they responded: "We don't know." To his credit, the farmer went on to say: "I think the girls will work at home when they come back from school, and this may take their time from studying."[11]

There are roles for some of the educated women in Kossoye. The director of the school from 2004 to 2006 was a 26-year-old Kemant woman who established a reputation as an effective administrator. Since the expansion of the teaching staff in the 1990s more women have been teachers, although males predominate. The community health workers and health post staff are predominantly women. The secretary for the chairman of the local government was a woman.

But education complicates a woman's marriage prospects. There are two parts to this problem. The first is that farming remains the single largest occupation and the bedrock of the local and most household economies. The second is that men with land tend to be uneducated and most educated women do not want to marry uneducated men. Teshome noted, after both his wife and daughter shyly acknowledged that educated girls will not agree to marry uneducated farmers: "It is true that the educated woman does not marry the uneducated man. This can be a problem. At any rate, the uneducated man will look for an uneducated woman. The educated woman will leave Kossoye and go to Gondar or someplace where she can find an educated man."[12] In 1998 the male school director said that educated girls "show contempt" for uneducated men. "Educated girls want to be married to educated men. She doesn't even want to be married to a rich man without education."[13]

Although educated children will presumably find opportunities outside of Kossoye, there is special concern about the girls. In 1994, a nun who had raised her four nieces and nephews after their parents' premature deaths said: "The one who is not educated and literate is similar to walking in the dark. My children are not in the dark. They are educated. If the government governs well, they will know what to do."[14] In discussing this situation in 1998, Kes Sisay said: "The boys can go everywhere, can work and live without personal problems. But the girls, even though they are educated, will face many problems. One, because they are many, there will be many who are jobless. Two, if they go around like the boys, they will have difficulties in their lives and will not get… husbands. They will have marriage problems. They will have job-getting problems. When I compare girls and boys, I see in the future, the girls' problems will be more than the boys' problems."[15]

The Market

In 1994 one schoolteacher noted, "Before five or six years [ago], if you ask for food or bread (*injera*), people will give it freely. But these days no one will give you freely. This is a very, very big change."[16] In fact, the change was hardly complete in 1994. The older generation preferred that Kossoye remain a closed community of subsistence farmers. The younger generation advocated an open community with a market.

In 1998 the leader of the older generation was Tagele, Taye's younger brother. Then 80 years old and a lifelong farmer, Tagele had some modern ideas. He deeply regretted never attending school. He had educated four of his six children and felt "very, very sad not to teach my oldest two daughters." Three of his children became successful modern people. His one son worked as a health assistant in a government clinic in Addis Zemen, about 100 kilometers away. A daughter who stayed in Kossoye married the school director. His youngest daughter finished high school, married, and moved to Azezo, a military town outside Gondar.[17]

Yet Tagele preferred the old way of life. The experiences of losing two houses (see chapter five) and his best land may have reinforced his conservatism. When interviewed in 1998, he explained: "We are farmers, country people....Markets are only advantageous for traders and retailers." He went on to make three points: First, Gondar and Ambaghiorgis "are not far away," thus not inconvenient for farmers. Second, "if there is a market, thieves and bandits will be here." Third, "our wives will take our grains to the market. Within a short time we will run out of food and we will be in trouble. If a market comes, we will have famine."[18]

On the other side were the pro-market, modern men. One of Taye's grandsons was listening as his great uncle Tagele stated his arguments and responded: "The existence of the market is essential. What we see in other towns can be available here if we have a market." The nephew wanted pharmacies, schools, shops, and opportunities for business.[19] The school director concurred. "Most of the community is poor," he said. "With a market they can work here and make a better life....If a market is present, I will have a place to eat and a hotel to stay at. It will also help the students."[20]

Kes Sisay was caught between his uncle's and son's positions. In 1994 he had opposed bringing a market to town, because "I was thinking that intoxicators, drunkards, robbers and thieves would come here. That was what I worried about." By 1998 his position changed: "I am very eager to see that Kossoye has a market."[21]

It would seem that Kes Sisay's position changed as he witnessed the modern generations' life challenges. All of his children attended primary school, and some went on to high school in Ambaghiorgis. Some moved away to work as policemen, soldiers, and traders. Three worked in neighboring Sudan. But most of them returned home, at least for a while, because of unemployment or marital problems. As Kes Sisay put it, life has become "hand to mouth." Since the older children do not have jobs, he said, there is "more burden on me."[22] A young modern shopkeeper with a 12th grade education and one child noted in 2005 that "maybe 40% [of the young people] leave Kossoye for school or work. The unemployed stay around in the beer house, as *lumpen*, drinking and gambling. This is a problem."[23] Another modern man, in his 30s, also a 12th grade graduate, agreed: "Lots of young people are without work.... They fight.... Idle people are the biggest problem."[24]

One of the ironies of the traditionalist-modern debate about having a market is that, when police service came into Kossoye in 2006 it was not because of thieves from the lowlands, but thieves from within: unemployed young people. In the 1965 census "the unemployed" was not recognized as a separate occupational category. It was assumed that there was enough work for everyone. In the 1994 census, students from the Gondar College of Medical Sciences (the successor to the Haile Sellassie I Public Health College) identified 17 (1.7%) unemployed persons. By the time of the 2004 census the number of unemployed had increased to 59 (4.3%).

In industrial societies this would be a relatively low rate of unemployment, but in Kossoye it is a significant problem, because most of the unemployed are educated people under 30 years of age. Kes Sisay put it this way in 2005: "The biggest problem [in Kossoye] is unemployment, especially of the educated."[25] When "parents see that even grade 12 graduates are unemployed, they ask [reported one teacher], what is the purpose of sending our children to school?"[26] Other parents realize that education is no guarantee of employment but that there is really no alternative for their children, since obviously they cannot farm.

Unemployment has led to questions about the new social order in Kossoye. In the 1960s no one thought that educated children would become thieves and bandits, preying on their own community. At that time people did not imagine that children in their twenties and thirties could be without land, jobs, or families. But over the past several years people have come to understand that too many people without land or work leads to insecurity for the community as a whole. In 2005 the Kossoye school lost many of its library books, stolen and sold on the market, apparently by unemployed graduates. The grain storage facility was also robbed at gunpoint in 2005. Kossoyans suspect that the culprits are local unemployed youths rather than thieves from the lowlands.

Health, Wealth, and Family

The central goal of the College students and faculty who came to Kossoye in 1963 was to empower and assist the local people to improve their lives. Forty-four years later, is it possible to say whether life is better? The answer is complicated.

One way in which life is better is that more people have had an opportunity for some education. Before 1965 Kossoye had no public school. Virtually everyone in town was illiterate. Now most Kossoyans are literate and the local school is a dynamic institution that wins awards in academics and sports. Many children travel long distances to study in

Kossoye. Some families have settled in town because of the school. Alumni go on to high school, college, government jobs, and even to study and work in the United States and Europe. Some send money back to the school, their families, and the neighborhood church. In retrospect building the school did more than anything else to assure Kossoye's growth as a town.

In health there are have been areas of improvement. Family planning services are available and used by about 20% of fertile-aged women in the Kossoye *kebele*. Rates of intestinal parasites are much lower than in the 1960s. Diseases connected to poor personal hygiene are also less common, because people are cleaner. Educated children in the eighth grade understand the importance of limiting family size.

Kossoyans are also less vulnerable to acute starvation. In *The African Poor: A History* (1987) John Illife notes that one benefit of globalization that has characterized the post-World War II world is that episodes of extreme poverty resulting from famine have been ameliorated because of improved transportation and communication.[27] That is certainly true in Kossoye. The Great Famine of the 1890s was much harsher than the famine of 1984-85, because of the assistance of the international community.

Yet there are also ways in which life is *not* better. In the 1960s Kossoyans distinguished between neighbors who were poor and wealthy: there were discernible advantages that made some families more secure than others. Now almost everyone identifies themselves as poor (*deha*). This sense of impoverishment comes from greater awareness, as a result of print media, radio, and television, but it also is a result of severe land shortage. Now children cannot count on sustaining their families through agriculture, and even the children who have access to land will farm less than one hectare, when in the 1960s their grandfathers often farmed 4 or even 10 hectares.

Another way in which life is not better in Kossoye is that educated unemployed males and females are now a significant statistical category in Kossoye society. This is related to land shortages, since parents send their children to school as an alternative to agricultural employment on family land. But it is also related to a lack of non-agricultural opportunities. Now the community needs police protection from its own educated unemployed. Not only do the *lumpen* drink and carouse, they also resort to theft, making the community less secure.

Finally, Kossoyans worry about the local-national-global dynamics which have so negatively impacted them over the past fifty years. They understand the consequences of far-off events. They understand that human society in their locality is in a sustainability crisis quite unlike anything that their grandparents experienced or expected. They are not sure what to do.

Remedies

Kossoye is on the verge of becoming a market town. No doubt there will be new businesses, especially aimed at meeting the needs of lowlanders. No doubt these new opportunities for nonagricultural employment will also allow more of the modern generation to find work. But making life in Kossoye better for the modern generation will require serious effort, on the local, national, and even international levels. As Taylor-Ide and Taylor argue in *Just and Lasting Change: When Communities Own Their Futures*, the best prospects for positive change come when local, national, and international initiatives work in concert.[28]

In the past fifty years there have been periods of local-national-international synergy in Kossoye, but it seems that Kossoyans have suffered more than they have benefited from their connections to the rest of the world. Several things need to happen for this not to be the case in the 21st century.

At the international level, it is remarkable that 147 world leaders signed the Millennium Development Goals to end extreme poverty by 2025. Kossoyans will likely benefit from such international initiatives, but there are serious questions about whether this help will be steady and sustainable. In *The End of Poverty: Economic Possibilities for Our Time*, Jeffrey D. Sachs explains what could happen if the world's richest countries lived up to their promises to devote 0.7% of their gross domestic products to development in the poorest parts of the world.[29] But in the seven years since the millennium declaration, most of the world's wealthiest nations (including the United States) have failed to live up to their promises. One positive outcome of this United Nations-led initiative is the careful thought that has gone into defining basic living standards for all the world's peoples.

In Ethiopia since 1991 the government has focused on a development agenda that is more in concert with global capitalism, in programs that combine market economics and government ownership of land. Initiatives include:

- Increasing trade, so that a dynamic urban/commercial/industrial sector develops which can take some pressure off of overpopulated rural areas like Kossoye.
- Improving access to family-planning technologies, so that fertility declines significantly below the current five children per woman—an obvious necessity in a context of increasing malnutrition.
- Encouraging the Ethiopian diaspora to invest money and time (a partial reversal of the "brain drain") in their homeland.
- Expanding educational opportunities, especially in colleges and universities.
- Encouraging Ethiopians to increase export of cereals, a goal suggested by Sachs in the *End of Poverty* and now also supported by USAID.

- Participating in the United Nations' Millennium Development Goal campaign by evaluating and reporting on achieving benchmarks of poverty reduction.

Privatization of land is discussed but not on the horizon in Ethiopia, and it is not clear that under present circumstances (with severe land shortages and inadequate nonagricultural job opportunities) that such a policy would be wise.

At the local level, there are several actions Kossoyans can take to improve their lives and strengthen their community. The expansion of the local economy will provide opportunities for the educated and the landless. The market in Kossoye will attract more country people for supplies and services. Electricity will provide more opportunities for illumination, nighttime entertainment, refrigeration, and communication. More townspeople will be able to make a living outside of farming.

Development of basic public health infrastructure that was begun in the 1960s, discontinued during the *Derg*, and restarted in the 1990s remains a high priority. Additional protected wells and springs can be built to provide better access to clean water. Every house should have a latrine. New houses should be built with ventilation and simple improved technology for cooking.

Family-planning remains a high priority, although Kossoyans will continue to be dependent on the national and international communities for supplies. In recent years Kossoyans have demonstrated an understanding of the problems caused by having six, seven, or more children. It is not clear that the national government will undertake the sort of vigorous public education campaign needed to make progress in limiting family size.

Kossoyans can adopt land use strategies that balance needs for locally produced food, cash crops (eucalyptus), and the sustainability of their highland ecosystem. Eucalyptus nurseries have evolved as a way of coping with land shortages, and they have provided most Kossoyans with some cash. More families are planting potatoes as a hedge against famine, alongside or in place of the barley used for making beer. A number of people in the community (mostly women) have become successful vegetable gardeners. Land use and agriculture are topics that children study in school. And of course Kossoyans are also seeing nonagricultural land uses, like the creation of a marketplace on a central meeting place.

As they become more firmly connected to the national electric grid, Kossoyans will also face the challenge of assessing appropriate technology so that they do not become more vulnerable to the vicissitudes of the global economy, and particularly energy prices. In Sachs' Millennium Villages, inputs such as community pickup trucks and chemical fertilizers are provided to increase yields and access to markets.[30] It is not clear that this strategy makes sense in Kossoye, given the high costs of fossil-fuel-based agriculture and transportation. But there are many innovations that are economically and culturally appropriate.

Becoming a market town will increase the challenge of creating a positive civic culture in a pluralistic environment. This is not a new problem; Kemant, Bete Israel, Amharas, Tigrays, Oromos, and others have lived together in the area for many, many years. But now the five parish churches will have to accommodate Muslims, Pentecostals, television, and a global media culture that is not always positive.

Of course, the local-national-international connections which we have witnessed over the past 44 years will continue in Kossoye into the future. We hope that the synergies from these connections will help Kossoyans and other communities like theirs improve the quality of their lives.

Notes

1. See for example Harold G. Marcus, *A History of Ethiopia* (Berkeley: University of California Press, 19914); Paul B. Henze, *Layers of Time: A History of Ethiopia* (New York: Palgrave Macmillan, 2000); Sarah Vaughan and Kjetil Tronvoll, *The Culture of Power in Contemporary Ethiopian Political Life*, Sidastudies No. 10 (Stockholm: Swedish International Development Cooperation Agency, 2005); Bahru Zewde, *A History of Modern Ethiopia 1855-1991*, Second Edition (Addis Ababa: Addis Ababa University Press, 2002); Bahru Zewde and Sigfried Pausewang, editors, *Ethiopia: The Challenge of Democracy from Below* (Addis Ababa: Forum for Social Studies, 2002); Abebe Zegeye and Siegfried Pasuewang, editors, *Ethiopia in Change: Peasantry, Nationalism and Democracy* (London: British Academic Press, 1994).

2. Jan Nederveeen Pieterse, *Globalization & Culture: Global Melange* (Lanham: Rowman & Littlefield Publishers, Inc., 2004).

3. Of course, not all the young people in Kossoye are equally integrated into modern practices and culture. About half of the children in the community go to school. The others spend their days fetching water and herding cattle. About half the people under 30 have at least minimal literacy acquired at school or during one of the literacy campaigns. The other half can neither read nor write. About half of the young people have modern ideas about careers and marriage. The others have more traditional views about their careers and family prospects. The modern ones read the newspapers. The traditional ones learn from their elders. The modern ones hope to find non-agricultural work. The traditional ones have some security, although they usually live with parents and kin.

4. See for example, Abbebe Kileysus, "Cosmologies in Collision: Pentecostal Conversion and Christian Cults in Asmara," *African Studies Review*, Volume 49, number 1 (April 2006): 75-92.

5. For details on Taye's inheritance and dowry see chapter two.

6. Interview 12, February 16, 1994.

7.   Interview 5, February 16, 1994.

8.   Interview 71, January 5, 2005.

9.   Interview 51, April 28, 1998.

10. Interview 51, April 28, 1998.

11. Interview 48, May 1, 1998.

12. Interview 48, May 1, 1998.

13. Interview 13, February 17, 1994.

14. Interview 4, February 17, 1994.

15. Interview 47, April 29, 1998.

16. Interview 13, February 17, 1994.

17. Interview 21, February 18, 1994.

18. Interview 51, April 28, 1998.

19. Interview 51, April 28, 1998.

20. Interview 50, April 28, 1998.

21. Interview 47, April 29, 1998.

22. Interview 70, January 5, 2005.

23. Interview 68, January 4, 2005.

24. Interview 61, January 4, 2005.

25. Interview 70, January 5, 2005.

26. Interview 13, February 17, 1994.

27. John Iliffe, *The African Poor: A History* (Cambridge: Cambridge University Press, 1987), chapter one.

28. Daniel Taylor-Ide and Carl E. Taylor, *Just and Lasting Change: When Communities Own Their Futures* (Baltimore: Johns Hopkins Press, 2002), chapter two.

29. Jeffrey D. Sachs, *The End of Poverty: Economic Possibilities for Our Time* (New York: Penguin Books, 2005), 1-4.

30. Sachs, *The End of Poverty*, 233-236.

2005: Hanging out at the teahouse.

2005: A young man reads an announcement, posted on a local shop, regarding the May 2005 elections.

2004: The Kossoye school, grades 1-8.

2004: Students in a classroom.

2005: Students have access to clean water at the school. The pump, made in India, was provided by the United Nations.

2005: People waiting for treatment at the Health Post.

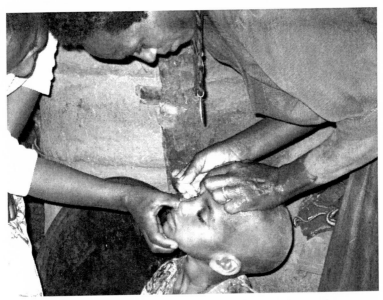

2005: Mother applying Tetracycline Eye
Ointment during mass treatment.

2005: A young mother talking inside her home
with the Community Health Worker.

2005: The CHWs (community health workers),
members of the modern generation.

GLOSSARY

❖ ❖ ❖

aja	oats
aleka	a chief leader, as at a local church
ata	indigenous tree
atbia dangna	a local judge (feudal era)
ater	peas
balabbat	a district leader from the nobility (feudal era)
baqela	beans
balezar	a possessed person and healer
bozie	grain
buda	a person with an evil eye
chika shum	a local leader and tax collector (feudal era)
chikanet	the local area administered by the *chicka shum*
chewa	a well-mannered person, or an illiterate; also a "pure race" (including from disease)
debtera	a learned person in the Ethiopian Orthodox Church
dega	highlands
Derg	the committee, also used to refer to the "Coordinating Committee of the Armed Forces" from 1975-1991
doqma	an indigenous tree

endod	an indigenous plant used for soap and schistosomiasis control
fidel	the Amharic alphabet
Geez	the language of the Ethiopian Orthodox Church
getem	indigenous tree
girar	acacia tree
gotera	a bin for storing cereals.
habtam	a rich man
hakeem	a medical doctor, health professional, or teacher
injera	a flat bread that is a staple of the Central and Northern Ethiopian diet
kalitcha	traditional spiritual healer, shaman, junior leader/teacher (Muslim)
kebelle	smallest political unit
kene	poems with hidden meanings
kes	priest
kole	spirits
kola	low lands
kosso	an indigenous tree with fruit used for treating tapeworms
kuna	a unit of measurement for grain, about 10 kilograms
madiga	a unit of measurement for grain, about 5 kilograms
makuannent	nobility (feudal era), officers
Pentes	slang expression for Pentecostals
quomata and *sentara*	inherited diseases or disabilities, usually leprosy
quorafe	a beverage
rist	land rights

shambel	the supervisor of the *chicka shum* (feudal era); military rank (current)
senbete	community meeting in the church yard where eating, drinking and discussion of community issues takes place
sindi	wheat
tabot	a sacred facsimile of the arc of the covenant
tebel	holy water
tella	local beer
telsa	a kind of grain
tenqwai	fortune teller
teskar	a memorial service and/or feast held for the dead at various periods (7, 30, 40, 80 days, then 6 months, then annually for 7-14 years)
tind	a unit of land measurement, approximately ¼ hectare
tennied	a kind of grain
tukul	a round waddle and daub house with thatched roof
wambar	the religious/political leader of the Kemant people
weyra	olive tree
wogesha	traditional surgeon/ bonesetter
wereda	administrative unit above kebele, district government
yemeskel	belonging to the cross or related to church
zemetcha	a campaign, as in to reduce illiteracy or achieve military objectives

BIBLIOGRAPHY

❖ ❖ ❖

Primary Sources

The primary sources used in this book have derived from the interaction of the College and the community of Kossoye. During the years from 1963 to 2007 well over 100 students, faculty, and staff have worked in Kossoye, collecting data and writing reports. Demographic surveys conducted by students and staff from 1963 through 2005 provide the basis for the tables and statistical analysis. The authors and the University of Gondar have copies of the individual survey forms. Several unpublished papers that have been important sources of information are listed with other unpublished documents. Most of these documents are Dennis Carlson's field notes. These documents are in the authors' possession. Between 1994 and 2006 the authors (with the help of some of the individuals noted in the preface) conducted 92 formal oral history interviews with people from all walks of life in the village. Fifteen of these interviews were lost due to technical difficulties with the recording equipment. The remaining 77 interviews have been transcribed and are in the authors' possession. All the interviewees consented to having their interviews recorded and used in this book. At the suggestion of local elders, names are used only for the older generations (people over 50 years of age at the time of the publication of this book). Most of the named individuals are deceased.

Unpublished Papers

Alemayehu Abraha. "Health in the Low and High Socio-Economic Groups in Kossoye with a Brief Review on the History, Geography, and Economy." Haile Sellassie I Public Health College and Training Centre Gondar (Ethiopia). (1965).

_____. "Bacteriological Examination of Water in Kossoye." (1963).

_____. "Kossoye Cherima Protected Spring Water" (1965).

_____. "Notes on a Trip to Kossoye." (1965).

_____. "A Case Study on the Relationship of Innovation, Health, and Economy in a Traditional Family." (1965).

Amare Beyene. "Hyena Control." (1964).

Carlson, Andrew J. "The Crazy Old Man in the Sacred Grove: Kemant Religion in an Orthodox Christian Parish." Paper presented to the Mid-West Conference of the American Academy of Religion, Chicago, March 25, 2000.

Carlson, Dennis G. "A Study of Change in Health, Economic, and Social Patterns in a Traditional Rural Community in Northern Ethiopia (Kossoyge-Medhaneallem)." (April 11, 1964).

_____. "Traditional Rural Community Notes." (July 1964).

_____. "Economic Development for What?"

_____. "Field Notes." (1963-64).

_____. "Field Notes." (1965-66).

_____. "Field Notes." (1964-74).

_____. "Attitudes Towards Fertility." (1967).

_____. "Fertility Control Research, Kossoye Medhane Alem." (1967).

_____. "Oral Traditions as Historical Source Materials: A Set of Problems in the Philosophy of History, with a Hypothetical Case Study." (1970).

_____. "The Kossoye Story: A 30 Year Perspective." (November 1993).

Mulugeta Mengistu. "A Report on the Study of Charima & Ginjero Wuha." (August 1964).

Shabir Ismael. "Family Planning Survey in Gondar." (1994).

Tadelle Mengesha. "Report on Social and Psychological Patterns of People at Cherema and Zenjiro Wuha." (1964).

Tsegaye Tekle. "An Economic and Demographic Survey of Some Famine Refugees in Begemidir-Simien Province." (1966).

Secondary Sources

Abbebe Kileysus. "Cosmologies in Collision: Pentecostal Conversion and Christian Cults in Asmara." *African Studies Review*, Volume 49:1(April 2006): 75-92.

Abebe Zegeye, and Siegfried Pasuewang, eds. *Ethiopia in Change: Peasantry, Nationalism and Democracy.* London: British Academic Press, 1994.

Abir, Mordechai. *Ethiopia, The Era of the Princes: The Challenge of Islam and the Reunification of the Christian Empire 1769-1855.* New York: Praeger, 1968.

Bahru Zewde. *A History of Modern Ethiopia 1855-1974.* 2nd edition. Addis Ababa: Addis Ababa University, 2002.

_____. *Pioneers of Change in Ethiopia: The Reformist Intellectuals of the Early Twentieth Century.* Addis Ababa. Addis Ababa University Press, 2002.

Bahru Zewde, and Siegfried Pausewang, eds. *Ethiopia: The Challenge of Democracy from Below.* Uppsala: Nordiska Afrikainstituet; Addis Ababa: Forum for Social Studies, 2002.

Banfield, Edward C. *The Moral Basis of a Backward Society.* New York: The Free Press, 1958.

Barth, Fredrik, ed. *Ethnic Groups and Boundaries: The Social Organization of Culture Difference.* Long Grove, Illinois: Waveland Press, Inc., (originally published in 1969), 1998.

Bender, M. Lionel, ed. *Peoples and Cultures of the Ethio-Sudan Border-lands.* Monograph No. 10. East Lansing: African Studies Center and Michigan State University, 1981.

Carlson, Andrew J., and Dennis G. Carlson. "Villagization in a Growing Ethiopian Town: Kossoye, 1963-1998." *Northeast African Studies*, Vol. 5, No. 2 (New Series, 1998): 117-133.

Carlson, Dennis G. "Famine in History: With A Comparison of Two Modern Ethiopian Disasters," in Kevin M. Cahill, ed. *Famine.* Maryknoll, New York: Orbis Books, 1982.

Cipolla, Carlo M. *The Economic History of World Population.* Middlesex, England: Penguin Books, 1962.

Clapham, Christopher. *Transformation and Continuity in Revolutionary Ethiopia.* Cambridge: Cambridge University Press, 1988.

_____. "Controlling Space in Ethiopia," in Wendy James, Donald L. Donham, Eisei Jurimoto, Alessandro Triulzi, eds. *Remapping Ethiopia: Socialism & After.* Oxford: James Currey, 2002: 9-32.

Collins, Robert O. *The Nile.* New Haven: Yale University Press, 2002.

Crummey, Donald. *Land and Society in the Christian Kingdom of Ethiopia From the Thirteenth to the Twentieth Century.* Urbana and Chicago: University of Illinois Press, 2000.

Easterlin, Richard A., ed. *Population and Economic Change in Developing Countries.* Chicago and London: University of Chicago Press, 1980.

Erlich, Haggai, and Israel Gershoni, eds. *The Nile Histories, Cultures, Myths.* Boulder, Colorado: Lynne Rienner Publishers, 2000.

Erlich, Haggai. *The Cross and the River: Ethiopia, Egypt and the Nile.* Boulder: Lynne Rienner, 2002.

Feierman, Steven, and John M. Janzen, eds. *The Social Basis of Health & Healing in Africa.* Berkeley: University of California Press, 1992.

Foster, George M. *Traditional Cultures and the Impact of Technological Change.* New York: Harper and Brothers, 1962.

_____. *Tzintzuntzan: Mexican Peasants in a Changing World* (reissued with changes). Prospect Heights, Illinois: Waveland Press, Prospect Heights, Illinois, 1967, 1979, 1988.

Foster, George M. et. al., eds. *Long-term Field Research in Social Anthropology.* New York: Academic Press, 1979.

Gamst, Frederick C. *The Qemant: A Pagan-Hebraic Peasantry of Ethiopia.* New York: Holt, Rinehart and Winston, 1969.

_____. *Peasants in a Complex Society.* New York: Holt, Rinehart and Winston, 1974.

Garrison, Fielding. *An Introduction to the History of Medicine* 4th Edition. Philadelphia: W. B. Saunders, 1966.

Greenfield, Richard. *Ethiopia: A New Political History.* New York: Frederick Praeger, 1965.

Haider, Jemal, and Hana Neka Tibeb. "Xerophthalmia in children of Torbayo, West Hararghe." *Ethiopian Journal of Health Development* Vol.12:1(1998): 39-43.

Halliday, Fred, Maxine Molyneux. *The Ethiopian Revolution.* London: Verso Books, 1981.

Hahn, Peter L., and Mary Ann Heis, eds. *Empire and Revolution: The United States and the Third World Since 1945.* Columbus, OH: The Ohio State University Press, 2001.

Hancock, Graham. *The Sign and the Seal: A Quest for the Lost Ark of the Covenant.* New York: Touchstone, 1992.

Henze, Paul B. *Layers of Time: A History of Ethiopia.* New York: St. Martin's, 2000.

Hoben, Allan. *Land Tenure among the Amhara of Ethiopia: The Dynamics of Cognatic Descent.* Chicago: The University of Chicago Press, 1973.

Hoffman, Elizabeth Cobbs. *All You Need Is Love: The Peace Corps and the Spirit of the 1960s.* Cambridge: Harvard University Press, 1998.

_____. "Decolonization, the Cold War, and the Foreign Policy of the Peace Crops," in Peter L. Hahn and Mary Ann Heiss, eds. *Empire and Revolution: The United States and the Third World since 1945.* Columbus, OH: The Ohio State University Press, 2001: 123-153.

Holcomb, Bonnie K., and Sisai Ibssa. *The Invention of Ethiopia: The Making of a Dependent Colonial State in Northeast Africa.* Trenton, NJ: The Red Sea Press, 1990.

Iliffe, John. *The African Poor: A History.* Cambridge: Cambridge University Press, 1987.

James, Wendy, and Donald L. Donham, Eisei Kurimoto, Alessandro Triulzi, eds. *Remapping Ethiopia: Socialism and After.* London: James Currey, 2002.

Keller, Edmond J. *Revolutionary Ethiopia: From Empire to People's Republic.* Bloomington: Indiana University Press, 1988.

Kidane Mengisteab. "New Approaches to State Building in Africa: The Case of Ethiopia's Ethnic-Based Federalism." *African Studies Review* Vol. 40, No. 3(1997): 111-133.

Kloos, Helmut, and Zein Ahmed Zein, eds. *The Ecology of Health and Disease in Ethiopia.* Boulder: Westview Press, 1993.

Knutson, Andie L. *The Individual, Society, and Health Behavior.* New York: Russell Sage Foundation, 1965.

Knutsson, Karl-Eric. *Authority and Change: A Study of the Kallu Institution Among the Macha Galla of Ethiopia.* Goteborg: Etnografiska Museet, 1967.

_____. "Possession and Extra-institutional Behavior." *Ethnos* 40: I-IV (1975): 244-272.

_____. "Dichotomization and Integration," in Fredrik Barth, ed. *Ethnic Groups and Boundaries: The Social Organization of Culture Difference.* Long Grove, Illinois: Waveland Press, Inc, 1998 reissue of 1969 edition: 86-100.

Korten, David C. *Planned Change in a Traditional Society Psychological Problems of Modernization in Ethiopia.* New York: Praeger Publishers, 1972.

Kuznets, Simon. "Recent Population Trends in Less Developed Countries and Implications for Internal Income Inequality," in Richard A. Easterlin, ed. *Population and Economic Change in Developing Countries.* Chicago and London: University of Chicago Press, 1980.

Levine, Donald N. *Wax and Gold: Tradition and Innovation in Ethiopian Culture.* Chicago: The University of Chicago Press, 1965, 1972. Midway reprint edition, 1986.

_____. *Greater Ethiopia: The Evolution of a Multiethnic Society.* 2nd edition. Chicago: The University of Chicago Press, 1974, 2000.

Marcus, Harold G. *A History of Ethiopia.* Berkeley: University of California Press, 1994.

Marcus, Cressida. "Imperial Nostalgia: Christian Restoration & Civic Decay in Gondar," in Wendy James, Donald L. Donham, Eisei Jurimoto, Alessandro Triulzi, eds. *Remapping Ethiopia: Socialism & After.* Oxford: James Currey, 2002: 239-256.

McCann, James C. *People of the Plow: An Agricultural History of Ethiopia, 1880-1990.* Madison: The University of Wisconsin, 1995.

McKeowan, Thomas. "Food, Infection, and Population," in Robert I. Rotberg and Theodore K. Rabb, eds. *Hunger and History: The Impact of Changing Food Production and Consumption Patterns on Society.* Cambridge: Cambridge University Press, 1983.

McClelland, David C. *The Achieving Society.* New York: Irvington Publishers, Inc, 1961, 1971.

Melkie Edris, Getnet Erakil. "The Prevalence of Low Birth Weight Delivery in Gondar Region, Northwest Ethiopia." *Ethiopian Journal of Health Development* Vol. 10:3 (1996): 149-152.

Merera Gudina. *Ethiopia: Competing Ethnic Nationalism and the Quest for Democracy, 1960-2000.* Addis Ababa: Chamber Printing House, 2003.

Messing, Simon D. *The Target of Health in Ethiopia.* New York: MSS Information Corporation, 1972.

Myrdal, Gunnar. *Asian Drama: An Inquiry into the Poverty of Nations.* 3 vols. New York: Pantheon, 1968.

_____. *Economic Theory and Underdeveloped Regions*. London: University Paperbacks, 1957.

Ofcansky, Thomas P., and LaVerle Berry, eds. *Ethiopia: a Country Study*. 4th edition. Washington, D.C.: Federal Research Division, Library of Congress, 1993/1991.

Oliver, Roland and J. D. Fage. *A Short History of Africa*. New York: New York University Press, 1962, 1964.

Pankhurst, Alula. "Surviving Resettlement in Wellegga: The Qeto Experience," in Wendy James, Donald L. Donham, Eisei Jurimoto, Alessandro Triulzi, eds. *Remapping Ethiopia: Socialism & After*. Oxford: James Currey, 2002: 133-150.

Pankhurst, Richard, ed. *Travellers in Ethiopia*. London: Oxford University Press, 1965.

_____, ed. *The Ethiopian Royal Chronicles*. Addis Ababa: Oxford University Press, 1967.

_____. *The History of Famine and Epidemics in Ethiopia Prior to the Twentieth Century*. Addis Ababa: Relief and Rehabilitation Commission, 1985.

_____. *An Introduction to the Medical History of Ethiopia*. Asmara, Eritrea: The Red Sea Press, 1990.

_____. "The Great Ethiopian Famine of 1888-1892: A New Assessment." *Journal of the History of Medicine and Allied Sciences* Vol. 21(1966): 95-124, 271-294.

Paul, Benjamin D., ed. *Health, Culture and Community: Case Studies of Public Reactions to Health Programs*. New York: Russell Sage Foundation, 1955.

Peet, Richard, with Elaine Hartwick. *Theories of Development*. New York: The Guildford Press, 1999.

Pieterse, Jan Nederveeen. *Globalization & Culture: Global Melange*. Lanham: Rowman & Littlefield Publishers, Inc., 2004.

Pilote, Louise, and George Olwit, Gebreselassie Okubagzi, Charles Larson. "Community based nutritional study: Geruke Jimate Peasants Association, Illubabor Region, Ethiopia." *Ethiopian Journal of Health Development* Vol. 5:1 (1991): 25-28.

Potter, Jack M. May N. Diaz, and George M. Foster, eds. *Peasant Society: A Reader.* Boston: Little, Brown and Company, 1967.

Rostow, W.W. *The Stages of Economic Growth: A Non-Communist Manifesto.* Cambridge: Cambridge University Press, 1960.

Rotberg, Robert I., and Theodore K. Rabb, eds. *Hunger and History: The Impact of Changing Food Production and Consumption Patterns on Society.* Cambridge: Cambridge University Press, 1983.

Rubenson, Sven. "The Lion of the Tribe of Judah, Christian Symbol and/ or Imperial Title." *Journal of Ethiopian Studies* Vol. III, No.2 (1965): 75-85.

_____. *The Survival of Ethiopian Independence.* London: Heinemann, 1976.

_____, ed. *Acta Aethiopica, Volume I, Correspondence and Treaties 1800-1854.* Chicago: Northwestern University Press, 1987.

_____, ed. *Acta Aethiopica, Volume II, Tewodros and His Contemporaries 1855-1868.* Addis Ababa: Addis Ababa University Press, 1994.

Sachs, Jeffrey D. *The End of Poverty: Economic Possibilities for Our Time.* New York: Penguin Books, 2005.

Selinus, Ruth, and Guenet Awalom, Abeba Gobezie. "Dietary Studies in Ethiopia II: Dietary Pattern in Two Rural Communities in N. Ethiopia; A Study with Special Attention to the Situation in Young Children." *Acta Societatis Medicorum Upsaliensis* LXXX (1971): 1-2.

Spruyt, Dirk et. al. "Demonstration & Evaluation Project Ethiopian Health Center Program." *Ethiopian Medical Journal* Vol. 5, No. 3 (1967): 35-36.

Taddesse Tamrat. "Processes of Ethnic Interaction and Integration in Ethiopian History: The Case of the Agaw." *Proceedings of the Ninth International Conference on Ethiopian Studies* Volume 6 (1986): 192-205.

Taylor-Ide, Daniel & Taylor, Carl E. *Just and Lasting Change: When Communities Own Their Futures.* Baltimore: The Johns Hopkins University Press, 2002.

Tesfaye Teshome. "Is Eucalyptus Ecologically Hazardous Tree Species?" Retrieved December 15, 2006 from http//www.ettf.org.

Timotewos Genebo, and Woldemariam Girma, Jamal Haider, Tsegaye Demesse. "The association of children's nutritional status to maternal education in Zigbaboto, Guragie Zone, Ethiopia." *Ethiopian Journal of Health Development* Vol.13:1(1999): 55-62.

Ullendorff, Edward. *The Ethiopians: An Introduction to Country and People.* London: Oxford University Press, 1960.

_____. *Ethiopia and the Bible.* The Schweich Lectures of the British Academy, 1967. London: Published for the British Academy by the Oxford University Press, 1968.

Vaughan, Sarah, and Kjetil Tronvoll. *The Culture of Power in Contemporary Ethiopian Political Life.* Sida studies No. 10. Stockholm: Swedish International Development Cooperation Agency, 2003.

Wubney, Mulatu, and Yohannis Abate. *Ethiopia: Transition and Development in the Horn of Africa.* Boulder, Colorado: Westview Press, 1988.

Yemane Berhane, and Damen Haile Mariam, Helmut Kloos, eds. *Epidemiology and Ecology of Health and Disease in Ethiopia.* Addis Ababa: Shama Books, 2006.

Yohannes Fitaw, and Yemane Berhane, Alemayehu Worku. "Differentials of fertility in rural Butajira." *Ethiopian Journal of Health Development* Vol.17:1(2003): 17-26.

Zawditu Getahun, and Kalbessa Urga, Timotewo Genebo, Ayele Nigatu. "Review of the status of malnutrition and trends in Ethiopia." *Ethiopian Journal of Health Development* Vol. 15:2 (2001): 55-74.

Zein, Ahmed Zein and Alemayehu Worku. "The distribution of low birth weight in the Gonder Administrative Region, Northwestern Ethiopia." *Ethiopian Journal of Health Development* Vol. 5:2 (1991): 71-74.

Zelealem Leyew. *The Kemantney Language: A Sociolinguistic and Grammatical Study of Language Replacement.* Koln: Rudiger Koppe Verlag, 2003.

INDEX

❖ ❖ ❖

development theory and agenda
1, 16, 18, 202; *see also* Engels,
Foster, Levine, Marcus, Marx,
Marxist-Leninst, Myrdal,
Weber

Development Through Cooperation Campaign 110

Desta Shamebo 161

diarrhea 48, 82, 84, 89, 167

Dire Dawa, city of 136

disease 8, 9, 12, 44, 47, 66, 70, 79,
80, 82-84, 86, 92, 137, 163,
166, 167, 170, 173, 174, 200,
213, 214

dowry 41, 61, 62, 192

drought 49, 79, 87, 88, 91, 117,
118, 161, 165

*Economic Theory and Under-
developed Regions* (Myrdal) 17

education 5, 7-12, 14, 37, 64,
67, 70, 79, 85, 86, 105, 110,
114-116, 120, 121, 125, 146,
149-151, 165, 166, 172, 176,
177, 192, 194-196, 198, 199,
202, 203

Egypt 5, 29, 30, 80, 86, 87, 137

electricity 203

Elizabeth II (queen) 57, 67, 75, 187

emperor, of Ethiopia 2-5, 7, 9-11,
16, 17, 26, 31, 45, 57-59, 67,
69, 70, 81, 82, 89, 105-108

empire, Ethiopia as 4, 81

End of Poverty, The (Sachs) 202

Engels, Frederick 16

Environmental Health Program
189

*Epidemiology and Ecology of
Health and Disease in Ethiopia,
The* 166

Eritrea 1, 2, 7, 15, 107, 116, 117,
135, 138, 161

Eshete Bogale 39, 96, 113, 138,
139, 141, 163, 176, 177, 185

Ethiopia-McGill Public Health
Training Program 165

Ethiopian Nutrition Institute
90. *See also* Child Nutrition
Institute

Ethiopian Orthodox Christian
Church 5, 24, 31, 37, 47, 60,
127, 140, 149, 152, 176, 188,
213, 214

Ethiopian People's Revolutionary
Democratic Front (EPDRF)
123, 124, 135, 171, 174, 178

Ethio-Swedish Children's Clinic
90

ethnicity 23, 32-37, 137-153,
168, 169. *See also* Kemant,
Agew, Falasha, Humera Agew,
Bete Israel, Amhara, Tigrayan,
Oromo, Gurage, Somali, mar-
riage, language death

eucalyptus 45, 59, 64-68, 109,
113, 114, 116, 131, 143, 153,
157, 164, 185, 186, 188, 203,
204

nobility 3-7, 11, 17, 105, 106, 213, 214

North America 1, 9, 116, 117

North Gondar Zone 166, 174

North Korea 109

nutrition 86-92, 97, 165-169, 178; and stunting 166, 167, 169

occupations, non-agricultural 187, 190-196

Organization of African Unity (OAU) 3

Oromo 6, 7, 35, 204

Orthodox Christian 3, 23-26, 30-39, 136-152, 190. *See also* Ethiopian Orthodox Church

Paul, Benjamin 12

Peasant Association 111, 113, 120. *See also* Farmer's Association

peasants 3-7; *see also* Banfield, Foster, Levine

Pentecostals 139, 140, 190, 204, 214

People's Democratic Republic of Ethiopia, The 117

Persia 1

pharmacies 81, 144, 197

Point Four 8; *see also* United States Aid in Development

Political Element in the Development of Economic Theory, The (Myrdal) 17

population 1, 6, 17, 18, 25-27, 79, 91-95, 97, 105, 126, 159-163, 185, 190, 193; growth 17, 18, 79, 93-97, 160-163, 178; of Ethiopia 1, 6, 105, 126, 178, 179

poverty 70, 169, 200, 202, 203

pregnancy and childbirth 48, 83, 94-98

protected spring: *see* water

Provisional Government of Ethiopia 110

public health, theory and policy 8, 9, 12-18, 77-82, 84, 85, 93, 97, 116, 165, 170-172, 190, 203

Qemant: *See* Kemant

Qemant, A Pagan Hebriac Peasantry of Ethiopia, The (Gamst) 27, 28

Queen of Sheba 1, 3

Red Cross Nursing School 8

Revolution, 1974-1991 105-127, 142, 192; models of 106; and generational divide 188, 189

Riley, James C. 92; *see also* health transition

rist 34, 62, 111, 214; *See also* land, inheritance

Rostow, W.W. 16; *see also* development, modernization
rural community 23-49; *see also* peasant, agriculture, farming
Russell, H.B.L. 93
Russians 81, 106, 108, 109; and Red Cross 81

Sachs, Jeffrey D. 202, 204
Saudi Arabia 30
Save the Children 161, 165
school: *see* Kossoye school, education
"Scramble for Africa" 81
Scrimshaw, Nevin 79
Second World War 1-3, 8, 200
Shabbir Ismael 175
shambel 63, 113, 126, 215
Shashitu Zewde 94, 95, 109, 174, 175; *see also* family planning, intrauterine contraceptive device
Shewa 4
Sign and the Seal, The (Hancock) 149
Sisay Taye (Kes) 37, 77, 111, 112, 115, 121, 135, 137-139, 141, 143, 145, 147, 148, 157, 160, 162, 176, 196, 198, 199
slaves, descendants of 6, 45, 137
Smallpox 79-81
Solomonic Dynasty 1, 3, 127
Somalia, Somali 7, 107, 116
Soviet Union 16, 109, 116, 160

subsistence economy 16, 39-46
Sudan 7, 27, 31, 42, 44, 57, 116, 124, 137, 188, 198
Sweden, Swedish Government 12, 89, 90
Taddesse Tamrat 27
Tadelle Mengesha 37
Tagele Wubineh 32, 34, 55, 111, 112, 114, 119, 120, 132, 135, 138, 145, 162, 165, 195, 197
Taiwan 11
Tamirat Yigezu 52, 126
Tanzania 117
Taye Wubineh 34, 37, 44-46, 53, 59, 70, 75, 77, 85, 95-98, 109, 126, 132, 160, 163-165, 188, 197
Taylor, Carl E. 79, 201
Taylor-Ide, Daniel 201
teachers 7, 10, 11, 58, 59, 66, 67, 70, 71, 93, 106, 121-123, 126, 138, 139, 141, 142, 145, 149, 151, 152, 164, 177, 188, 193, 195, 196, 199, 214
Tesfaye Teshome 146, 148
Tewodoros (Emperor) 81, 105, 107
Thematic Apperception Tests (TAT) 68, 69
Tigray, Tigrayan 4, 6, 7, 38, 62, 66, 117, 123, 135, 137, 148, 151, 204
Towns: see Ambaghiorgis, Gondar, Kossoye

trachoma 79, 82, 86, 172, 173

traders 6, 39, 191, 197, 198

traditional healers and medicine 83-85, 148, 170

trees 34, 45, 59, 64-68, 84, 109, 113, 114, 116, 143, 147, 148, 153, 164, 188; *see also* eucalyptus

tuberculosis 82

Tzintzuntzan: Mexican Peasants in a Changing World (Foster) 13

unemployment 198, 199

United States of America 2, 8, 10, 12, 15, 65, 89, 116, 190, 200, 202; *see also* North America

University College 8; *see also* Addis Ababa University, Haile Sellasie I University

United Nations 160, 178, 202, 203, 209

United Nations International Children and Education Fund (UNICEF) 8, 82, 160

United States Assistance in Development (USAID) 8, 202

United States Embassy 65

United States International Committee on Nutrition for National Defense (ICNND) 89

United States Peace Corps 10, 11, 58, 69

University of Gondar 169, 172, 189. *See also* Haile Sellasie I Public Health College and Training Centre, the College, Gondar College of Medical Sciences

Uppsala University 90

usufruct 115, 192

variolation 81, 99

vaccination 172

vegetable gardens 164, 204; *see also* agriculture

village, villager 9, 14, 23, 24, 37-39, 42-46, 57, 59, 64-67, 69-71, 84, 85, 90, 93, 118, 120, 123, 124, 142, 150, 162, 184, 204; Millennium Villages 204; *see also* Cherema and Zinjero Wuha, Kossoye, Kossoyans, rural community

villagization 111, 117-120, 122, 125, 162, 169

vitamin A deficiency 88-91, 166; *see also* nutrition

Wambar Muluneh Mersha 147, 149, 152, 157

water 9, 23, 46, 48, 58, 67, 81, 83, 84, 86, 87, 94, 125, 131, 137, 164, 171, 173, 203, 209, 215